MINERS

Volume 8

True Tales of the Old West

Charles L. Convis

by

Charles L. Convis

Illustrated by Betsy McLeod
Cover by Mary Anne Convis

PIONEER PRESS, CARSON CITY, NEVADA

Library of Congress Catalog Card Number: 96-68502

ISBN 0-9651954-8-1 (Volume)
ISBN 0-9651954-0-6 (Series)

Printed by
KNI, Incorporated
Anaheim, California

CONTENTS

ILLUSTRATIONS

IMPORTANT BUSINESS FROM THE MOUNTAINS

James W. Marshall drifted around New Jersey woods and sawmills until he learned the millwright's trade. In 1834, when he was twenty-four, the girl Marshall loved jilted him. He went to Missouri where a second jilting soured him on women for life. He moved on to Oregon in 1844.

After a long, wet winter of carpentry, Marshall moved to California, getting a job with John Sutter at his fort on the American River. In 1846 he joined the California volunteers and fought in the Bear Flag Rebellion. Marine Lieutenant Archibald Gillespie, military commandant over Los Angeles, made Marshall his chief carpenter to remodel buildings for military use. When the war ended he went back to work for Sutter.

Sutter put Marshall in charge of building a water-powered sawmill in the timbered foothills east of the fort. Construction started in fall, 1847. Sutter hired Indians and Mormons, recently discharged from the Mormon Battalion, to help Marshall. By early January, 1848, the water-wheel was in place and ready to test.

Marshall led the cheers as the water was turned into the millrace. But the wheel did not turn fast enough to power the saw! Careful study revealed that the tailrace (the ditch that carried the water back to the river) would have to be deepened.

By late January, Marshall thought it was time for another test. In his inspection on Sunday evening the twenty-third, he saw quartz in the ditch.

"Where there's quartz, there might be gold," he said.

No one paid attention. Marshall, a dour, grumpy man, often talked about spiritual visions and hearing strange voices. As usual, he left the watergate open to flush debris out of the tailrace.

The next morning Marshall saw something shiny when he closed the watergate and drained the tailrace. He picked up the pieces — some of them as large as small peas. He pounded them on a flat rock and found them malleable, not brittle like fool's gold.

"Boys, I think I've found gold," he shouted. The men crowded around. Some of them tested the pieces with their teeth, but none had ever seen natural gold. They got a caustic solution of lye from the cook and dropped a small nugget in. The lye had no effect. Marshall, as honest as he was harsh, said he would show the particles to Sutter.

A few days later he walked in on Sutter, saying he had something to show him in private. Sutter was not surprised at

Marshall's suspicion that someone would overhear. The man was like that. Sutter got an apothecary's scale. They measured out enough of the yellow particles to match the weight of three silver dollars. Then, by immersing each side in water, they discovered that the flakes and nuggets had a much higher specific gravity than silver.

Sutter consulted an encyclopedia and tested with nitric acid. Finally he said, "I believe this is the finest kind of gold."

Marshall was excited. He and Sutter were equal partners in the mill. "We'll be rich," he said. "It's all along the tailrace."

Sutter wasn't so sure. They agreed to keep the news quiet so Sutter's other employees would not desert to prospect for riches.

What Sutter put in his diary that day may have been the greatest understatement of the century: "Mr. Marshall arrived from the mountains on very important business."

The workers at the mill stayed on the job after they were allowed to keep the gold they found in their off hours. Other Mormons found gold at Mormon Bar. Soon the word had spread, and Sutter was hard pressed to find men to work his mills and care for his businesses, crops, and livestock. Neither he nor Marshall ever got rich.

Marshall prospected in his off duty hours, but he worked hardest to keep the mill going. In December Sutter sold his share. Marshall's new partners got the mill back in operation. For a time, Marshall did well. But fights with miners who abused the Indians did him in. Marshall had always employed Indians and he treated them well. But sticking up for them got him into so much trouble that he eventually lost the mill.

Marshall tried prospecting with no success. Farming, furniture making, and winemaking followed with the same result. He went on a lecture tour, getting stranded in Kansas City without funds. Leland Stanford sent him a railroad pass so he could visit his family in New Jersey (the first time since his youth) and return to California.

The legislature voted Marshall two hundred dollars a month for two years. He set up a blacksmith shop, but he drank up most of the money. A smaller pension followed, but Marshall had to rely on the charity of friends. He ended his days trying to eke out a living with the blacksmith shop. He was found dead in his bed August 10, 1885. He was seventy-five years old. Five years later the state built a nine thousand dollar monument to him.

Suggested reading: Donovan Lewis, *Pioneers of California* (San Francisco: Scottwall Associates, 1993).

WHEN NEWS TRAVELED SLOWLY

John Sutter paid little attention when James Marshall showed him the yellow metal found at the lumber mill he was building, forty miles away. Sutter needed construction lumber for his ranch. He did not need another report of some small pocket of gold that would entice his workers to lay down their tools and walk off into the mountains. Just to be safe, though, Sutter sent two men to San Francisco to file a claim to the land where the "goald" was found. A week later, he went up to see for himself.

The first announcement of the discovery was published in San Francisco in *The Californian* on March 15. It said that thirty dollars' worth of gold had been found on the American River and brought to Sutter's ranch. "California, no doubt, is rich in mineral wealth," the paper said. "Great chanches here for scientific capitalists." But two more months would pass before there was much interest in San Francisco.

An April 1 letter, written by a soldier, carried the first news east. The letter was addressed to the *New York Herald,* who published it on August 19. The letter, unsigned, had been written by a member of the 1st New York Volunteer Infantry. The writer told how his regiment had sailed around Cape Horn on a six months' journey to California two years before. He told about the military situation in California during the War against Mexico, and about agricultural and mercantile prospects. Finally, he mentioned "the mines of gold, silver, quicksilver, saltpeter, coal, etc. which abound. I am credibly informed that a quantity of gold, worth thirty dollars, was picked up lately in a bed of a stream of the Sacramento. I would predict for California a Peruvian harvest of the precious metals, as soon as a sufficiency of miners can be obtained."

The unknown soldier's letter was in a pack of mail carried east by Kit Carson. The famous scout was accompanied by Lieutenant George Brewerton, who was being transferred from the Presidio in San Francisco to the 1st U. S. Infantry in Mississippi. Brewerton had also come to California with the 1st New York Volunteers. He did not know about the letter they were carrying. Brewerton wrote a book about the journey and never said a word about the discovery of gold in California. Of course, he left San Francisco a month before the rush to the mountains had started from that city.

The country paid no more attention to the unsigned

letter published in New York than the Californians did at first to the newspaper announcement there.

Lieutenant William Tecumseh Sherman, adjutant general at the Presidio and later famous for a Civil War march to the sea, wrote a report for President Polk. Sherman said that California was known to contain precious metals when it was acquired in February from Mexico.

"Recent discoveries render it probable that these mines are more extensive and valuable than was anticipated. Reluctant to credit the reports in general circulation as to the quantity of gold, the officer commanding our forces in California visited the mineral district in July last, for the purpose of obtaining accurate information on the subject. When he visited the country, there were about 4,000 persons engaged in collecting gold."

By the time the *Herald* published the soldier's letter in mid August, experienced miners were moving to California from Mexico. Later in the fall, men started coming from the Oregon country. By this time, San Francisco was a ghost town. Soon, two-thirds of the men in Oregon were gone. But no one in the East knew of these events.

Sherman's report left Monterey by courier at the end of August. The courier took a schooner to Peru and a British steamer back to Panama. After crossing the Isthmus, he got passage to Jamaica and, from there, to New Orleans. Then he telegraphed his report to the War Department. President Polk, tired of criticism about the recent war with Mexico, made the report the feature of his December 5 report to congress. Two days later, the courier reached Washington. He carried 230 ounces of gold which his commander at the Presidio had privately purchased. Gold fever swept the East, and the rush of 1849 was on!

Suggested reading: John W. Caughey, *The California Gold Rush* (Berkeley: University of California Press, 1948).

HOW THE COMSTOCK GOT ITS NAME

Silver produced from the Comstock lode in Nevada helped the Union government finance the Civil War. The deepest in the world at the time, Comstock mines began the nation's silver mining industry. How the lode got its name illustrates the luck and the lies that marked prospecting in the old West.

The story starts with the Grosch brothers, Allen and Hosea, of Reading, Pennsylvania, for they found the silver. Allen was twenty-four and Hosea twenty-two when they joined the 1849 gold rush to California. They sailed to Tampico, marched across Mexico, and learned that the contractor who had promised to carry their company on to San Francisco had absconded with the passage money. They raised enough money to ride steerage to San Francisco, arriving August 30. Hosea was so sick from dysentery and malaria that Allen had to nurse him for months before they could work.

Like most of the 49ers, the brothers were young, strong, and hardy. But they were also observant, industrious, and temperate. They knew something of chemistry and mineralogy. They got a quiet religious faith from their clergyman father.

After two years of little success, the brothers crossed the Sierras to prospect in Gold Canyon. They found indications of a silver vein, but had to return to California to raise money needed for further exploration. Saving every dollar possible from their California prospecting, they returned to Gold Canyon in fall 1856. They wrote their father:

"We found two veins of silver at the forks of Gold Canyon. One is a perfect monster. We have hopes almost amounting to a certainty of veins crossing the canyon at two other points."

On August 16, 1857, Allen wrote of their first assay. It showed $3500 per ton. Even discounting for optimism, they must have been close to the great lode, itself. They had also found other veins, as yet untouched.

Three days later Hosea accidentally stuck a pick into his foot. With no doctor in the camps, Allen did his best, but gangrene set in and Hosea died within two weeks.

Allen considered giving up everything in his grief. "I feel very lonely," he wrote his father. "But I shall go on. . . By Hosea's death you fall heir to his share. We have, so far, four veins. Three of them promise much."

By late November Allen had paid off all debts from Hosea's sickness and burial. He set off with a friend, Canadian prospector Richard Bucke, to cross the Sierras and winter in

HOSEA and ALLEN GROSCH

Nevada Historical Society

California.

Winter came early and hard, as it had eleven years earlier for the Donner-Reed emigrant party. Allen and Richard had to kill their burro for food as they struggled to the summit above Squaw Valley through waist-deep snow. Then a second storm hit. The snow was so soft they could not use their home-made snowshoes. Six days later Bucke wanted to lie down and die, but Allen insisted that they keep going as long as they could move. The next day they took from morning until noon to crawl less than a mile. Their eyes were closing from weakness when they heard a dog bark and saw smoke below them in the valley.

But the rescue came too late. Allen died after a saw and hunting knife amputation of both legs. Bucke lost all of one foot and part of the other. He returned to Canada, studied medicine in Europe, and became one of the world's leading psychiatrists.

Henry Comstock had been a trapper before he tried prospecting. But he was too lazy and drank too much to succeed at anything. He moved in to the Grosch Brothers' cabin and persuaded two Indians to work the claim the brothers had staked out. The Indians were almost as lazy as he, and they found nothing.

But Comstock, enjoying an evening ride over the hills, saw two Irishmen cleaning up their rocker on a newly-marked claim. On land so barren it couldn't keep a goat alive, Comstock convinced the astonished Irishmen that he had a homestead claim of 160 acres for a ranch and they were trespassers.

"But I'll leave ye be if you'll cut me and my friends, Finney and Penrod, in as equal partners," announced one of the West's biggest phonies.

So Patrick McLaughlin and Peter O'Riley, to keep the peace, became partners with Comstock, James Finney, and Emanuel Penrod. The city that grew out of the mining camp took its name from Finney's native state, Virginia.

O'Riley died insane. McLaughlin went to a pauper's grave. Finney, a drinker like Comstock, fell off his horse and died of a fractured skull. Penrod, who survived them all, ranched and prospected until he died. Comstock blew out his brains in a mining camp near Bozeman, Montana. But the name of the laziest, lyingest prospector in the old West stuck to the richest lode in the world.

Suggested reading: Eliot Lord, *Comstock Mining and Miners* (Berkeley: Howell-North, 1959).

CAVE-IN

When mines caved in, instant death was merciful. Patrick Price, twenty-eight, single, and a native of Ireland, was not so lucky. On October 5, 1867, he was working in the Chollar-Potosi Mine directly below D Street in Virginia City, Nevada. A faithful, honest, and industrious man, he had been working at the mine for eighteen months.

Patrick's partner was lucky. A few minutes before the early-morning cave-in, he had injured his leg and had to be taken out of the mine. Otherwise, he would have shared Patrick's fate.

The two men had been timbering close to a recent cave-in, that had swallowed up a store on the surface. Suddenly the earth under Patrick's feet for about fifty feet in each direction gave way. Patrick was drawn under by shifting earth and timbers, but he was not completely buried.

The deep roar and Patrick's cries for help brought other miners on the run. But the obvious instability of the earth and timbers and the extreme danger of more collapse prevented them from approaching closer than twenty feet.

Patrick begged piteously to be rescued, calling his comrades by name, although he could not see them in the darkness. The other miners talked to Patrick for two hours, trying to lessen his anguish, but they could not reach him. Once they soaked a ball of oakum with kerosene, lighted it, and rolled it down near Patrick so they could see better.

"I see the light," Patrick said, joyously. I'm glad you're coming for me boys."

They tried to get a rope down but the great mass of loose rock settled in upon Patrick. His voice, which had been weakening, was heard no more. Then more earth slid down from above, and all rescue efforts stopped.

Almost twenty months later, on May 27, 1869, they recovered Patrick's body. Other attempts had been made, but constant shifting of the treacherous ground had stymied the rescuers. Patrick's lower jaw, part of his right arm, and other small bones had been carried away by rats. The remaining flesh had mummified.

A large crowd came to Patrick's funeral at St. Mary's Catholic Church. His union escorted the body to its final place of rest.

Suggested reading: *Gold Hill Daily News*, October 7, 1867.

LESSONS FROM THE MINES

The Stuart brothers, Granville, 17, and James, 19, left their Iowa farm in 1852, traveling with their father to the California goldfields. They crossed Beckwourth Pass and stopped for a night at Bidwell's Bar, where John Bidwell had taken out one hundred thousand dollars in 1848 and 1849. Sam Neal did as well at his ranch, twenty miles northwest on Butte Creek. The Stuarts went on to Neal's.

Meals were a dollar each and the boys were anxious to prospect, so they left their father behind and traveled fifteen miles northeast to the Butte Mills camp. There they joined two young men, 18 and 19, who had been in California a year and proposed to prospect some dry gulches on Little Butte Creek.

Granville was thrilled with the country. Magnificent sugar pines towered three hundred feet high with smaller yellow pines, firs, cedars, oaks, madrones, and dogwoods below. Manzanita perfumed the air.

Granville enjoyed hunting deer and squirrels with his muzzle loader and a dog he had picked up on the trail. In fact, he once suggested to James that they could make more money by buying burros and packing deer meat into the gold camps. But it was mining they came to do and they stuck with it.

Granville was impressed with the "good-looking" Indians. Naked in summer, they wore only a tiny apron, made of wisps of grass, in winter. He said that in his eighteen-year-old innocence he thought he had strolled into the Garden of Eden. He enjoyed eating grasshoppers the Indians roasted for him.

The brothers learned some important lessons during their eighteen months in California. Back home in Iowa they had heard fire and brimstone sermons from Brother Briar, a circuit-rider who often stayed at the Stuart cabin. Afterward the boys would climb to their sleeping loft, their hair standing on end, to dream of devils carrying pitch forks. One evening Granville entered a California gambling hall to hear the music and watch the players. In the great, glittering room full of light, music, and excited gamblers, he saw Brother Briar dealing faro! That ended Granville's belief in hell fire.

The next summer the brothers threw in with another pair of miners. They dammed a creek with two parallel rock walls, filling between them with dirt carried down from the hills in sacks. They worked six weeks digging a canal to carry the water to their diggings. But the dam leaked, the new partners said they could never make it pay, and they abandoned their claims and split up. As the Stuart brothers suspected and confirmed later, their former partners returned to the ditch, working the claims successfully.

The brothers joined up with a friend to prospect some old dry gulch diggings that had been abandoned three years before when the pay streak was lost. They found the lost pay streak, but had no paper or pencil to mark their claim. They returned to their cabin, two miles away, intending to come back the next morning to put up the claim notice.

The next day was Sunday, and James and their friend decided to wash clothes.

"I think we ought to go back and put up the notice," Granville said.

"Don't worry," they said, laughing. "That place is dry as a bone. There won't be any one around there for at least two months when the rains start."

When they went back Monday morning, Tom Neal and several of his friends had staked notices, freezing out the three discoverers. Neal and his friends had been walking by on Sunday afternoon and saw where the pay streak had been uncovered. The Stuarts and their friend had left their tools on the ground, making the place easy to see!

Neal and his friends took out over twenty-five thousand dollars from their claims, while the brothers spent the winter making clapboards and shakes out of sugar pines.

The next spring the Stuart brothers moved north to what would become Montana. Their letter to a brother in Colorado touched off the Montana gold rush, although they profited no more from it than they had in California.

Both brothers served in the territorial legislature. James was the first sheriff of Missoula County. Granville became Montana's leading cattleman and one of the state's finest citizens. President Cleveland appointed him ambassador to Paraguay and Uruguay.

The brothers never forgot the lessons they had learned in California.

Suggested reading: Granville Stuart, *Prospecting for Gold* (Lincoln: University of Neb. Press, 1977).

A VICTIM'S VIEW OF THE GOLD RUSH

By the time he was seventeen Jose Fernandez had sailed from Spain to Peru and on to California. There he joined the frontier army, garrisoned at Yerba Buena (later called San Francisco) to keep Indians in check.

Fernandez, like all Spaniards, had difficulty with the Mexican government after it revolted from Spain. But the Mexicans allowed him to join their army and, by the time the Americans came, he had risen to captain. In 1849 Fernandez became alcalde (mayor) of San Jose, one of the few spaniards elected to office during American rule.

Fernandez' interview with historian Hubert Bancroft provides a rare record of the viewpoint of Spanish Californians on the gold rush.

"Gold was discovered," Fernandez said, "by Mormon laborers who had come to California with the well-known drunkard Samuel Brannan. They were building a sawmill for John A. Sutter, another drunkard of the first class.

"Many died of hunger and thirst in the stampede to the mines, and others at the hands of robbers. Robbers and murderers even pursued their victims into San Francisco and San Jose.

"No one knew how much gold was mined in 1848. Three thousand Indians invaded Tuolumne, El Dorado, and Calaveras Counties with no capital but their hands, their gold pans, and their bows and arrows. Yet they removed enough gold to keep themselves drunk for months. Then they reverted to lives of idleness and brutality. Tribes which, fifty years before, had counted their warriors by tens of thousands, almost became extinct.

"By the end of 1848 an aristocracy of lucky gamblers had taken over Sacramento. They soon became masters of the country, electing governors, senators, judges, and even the police. Sometimes they allowed an honest man to be elected to an office of little importance.

"Potatoes, which two years before brought a dollar a sack, were worth seventy-five cents a pound. Eggs were a dollar each. It cost you a half dollar every time you put a fork into your mouth. Furnished rooms could not be found. For two or three dollars a night one could sleep under the roof of a warehouse.

"During 1849 hundreds of foreign ships brought their citizens to California. Australia sent criminals, Italy musicians, Germany barbers and beer drinkers, England pugilists, France bullies and prostitutes, Mexico monte players, Chile sneak thieves and pickpockets, Peru malefactors, Ireland highway robbers, and the United States politicians and plotters and, now and then, a man of property with his followers of artisans and farmers.

"Every day many set out for the mines full of hope, and every day many returned to San Francisco, disgusted with the mines where they had wasted their time and contracted diseases. Rheumatism, fevers, and dysentery filled the hospitals and graveyards of San Francisco.

"Not only the passengers, but the captains and crews abandoned their ships to search for gold. By the middle of 1849 over one hundred and fifty large ships had been abandoned in San Francisco harbor. Some were converted into warehouses, others into hotels and boarding houses. Many were cut up into firewood.

"To fall sick was to die, since physicians were very few and they charged exorbitant fees. Public hospitals caused illness to persons who came to visit sick friends. The attendants were lame or one-armed sailors, who could find no other work at $100 a month. More than that could be made in a single day in the mines.

"The California legislature sent to the United States Senate a creature of the railroad monopoly. There was nothing so evil that the legislature would not do it."

Fernandez did have great praise for General Mariano Vallejo, member of the legislature, for Thomas Larkin, United States Consul, and for Dr. Robert Semple.

"Mexico, France and Peru sent an infinity of prostitutes who acquired much money. The French ladies of pleasure did not have to pay their passage. The French government, wanting to get rid of their impenitent Magdalens, conducted a lottery and used the profit to ship three hundred to California. The French women did more damage to public morals than did the Mexicans because they were more skilled in trapping the unwary. The Peruvian prostitutes were excellent dancers which helped in their entertainment of the miners.

"I am aware that what I say is contrary to what has been written about Fremont and his followers," Fernandez concluded. "But the history written by the victim does not altogether chime with the story of the victor since, from the time of Abel, it has been the custom to distort the facts so as to crown the conqueror with laurels which he has not deserved."

Suggested reading: Captain Jose Fernandez, "The Coming of the Forty-Niners" in Valeska Bari (Ed.) *The Course of Empire* (New York: Coward-McCann, Inc., 1931).

THE LUCK OF THE IRISH

Winfield Scott Stratton, like hundreds of other American boys born in 1848, was named for the old general, then enjoying great success in Mexico. With seven sisters and a mother who was always having babies, Winfield soon had enough of women. He left his Indiana home at twenty. Drifting west, he reached Colorado Springs in 1872.

Stratton set up a carpentry shop on Pike's Peak Avenue. A skilled craftsman, he soon had more work than he could handle. One of the houses he built was later famous as the home of Helen Hunt, author of *Ramona*.

Stratton was hot-tempered, almost neurotic. He did not like other people, and did not seem to enjoy life. By 1874 three business partnerships had ended in fights, and he was tired of carpentry. Like many others in Colorado Territory, he became a part-time prospector.

He spent $2800 and two months on a mining claim in the San Juan Mountains. All he brought back to Colorado Springs was some practical knowledge of prospecting.

But he liked the life. He enjoyed the quiet mountains and traveling with a burro. Burros did not talk back, argue, complain, overcharge, or make stupid demands. They just did what they were told. For the next seventeen years, Scott did carpentry in the winter to finance his summer prospecting.

In June, 1876, he married seventeen-year-old Zeurah Stewart after a short courtship.

"I think I'm pregnant, Winfield," Zeurah told him just days after the ceremony.

Stratton remembered why he hated women.

"I had nothing to do with it," he said at the end of his temper tantrum. He renounced their marriage, sent her back to her Illinois home, and never saw her again. Her son would be a young man before Stratton ever saw him.

Stratton concentrated his prospecting in the Cripple Creek area, west of Colorado Springs. He walked over the land, studying outcrops, picking up float rock for assays, digging here and there for samples, and tracing drainage courses. He talked to other prospectors and miners, took private courses, and studied mining operations, geology, and mineralogy. On July 3, 1891, he found a granite ledge which looked promising. The next day he staked the available ground in two claims, which he named the Independence and the Washington.

Almost two years later, despairing of ever finding paydirt, he accepted five thousand dollars from a San Francisco mining syndicate for a thirty-day, renewable option to buy the Independence. At that time, he had a shaft eighty-five feet deep, with four crosscuts.

He had abandoned one of the crosscuts a year before. When he moved his equipment out of the mine, he went into the abandoned crosscut to see if anything had been left behind. In moving a rusty drill that he had forgotten, he knocked a rock loose from the wall. Seeing a discoloration, he explored some more. After several hours of work, he was sure he had found a big vein. He put the debris back and backed out of the musty crosscut with his bags of samples.

After the assays, Stratton calculated that he had at least three million dollars worth of ore in sight! The option had until July 28 to run. The syndicate had its crews working steadily in the Independence. They obviously hadn't gone into the fourth crosscut. Would they now? Would they find the vein in one of the other crosscuts? The next few days were the most nerve-wracking of Stratton's life.

On July 27 L. M. Pearlman, the syndicate's representative, took Stratton to dinner at the Palace, the best hotel in Cripple Creek. They ate in front of a huge fireplace, pine logs burning brightly in the cool summer evening. Stratton was in a cold sweat for the entire meal.

"Cripple Creek isn't developing like people thought it would," Pearlman said.

"Really?"

"We haven't found enough yet to cover our option payment."

"Well."

"I was figuring to have the crew look into that abandoned crosscut tomorrow, but I hate to spend another day's wages."

Stratton could barely breathe.

"Look here Stratton, I want to leave town in the morning. How about taking back your option tonight?" He pulled the paper from his pocket and thrust it forward.

Stratton couldn't keep his hands from trembling. He nodded toward the fire. "Just toss it in the fire," he said, trying to keep his voice from shaking.

Cripple Creek became the world's greatest gold camp. It produced twice as much ore as the entire mother lode country in the Sierras. Winfield Scott Stratton was the first of its twenty-eight millionaires.

Suggested reading: Marshall Sprague, *Money Mountain* (Boston: Little, Brown and Company, 1953).

THREE PARTNERS

The two men walking down Harrison Avenue in Leadville, Colorado, in 1878 looked like tramps. August Rische, a Missouri shoemaker, and Theodore Hook, a Pennsylvania iron-puddler, had been searching for gold for several years. Both Germans, they had become friends in a fruitless quest for wealth.

"Maybe it's silver vee shutt hunt," Hook had suggested.

They continued past the oil-burning lights to a dark hill at the end of the street. A deserted cabin, its door open, appeared in front of them. Riche leaned in and struck a match.

"Py golly, Ted," he said, "a change in luck vee haff. Two bunks it hass unt some food for breakfast efen."

They found a half loaf of bread, a few pieces of bacon, and some tea leaves on a shelf. In twenty minutes they were sound asleep.

The next day, Sunday, April 21, was the brightest, warmest day of the spring. Hook and Rische rose early and built a fire outside the cabin. They used sticks to hold the bacon over their fire, letting the grease drip onto thick slices of bread. They washed their food down with warm tea, wiped their faces, and looked up at Fryer Hill, where Leadville's initial silver discovery had been made.

The two men, often working for wages to make ends meet, had become familiar with mineral formations. After tramping over the hill, they looked at each other and grinned.

"Py golly," Riche said, "I think a lot of silver vee gott."

"Ach, mein Gott, if only somebody to stake us a while yet vee could find."

They tried Edwin Harrison, owner of the smelter in Leadville. But Harrison was busy, and he sent the tramps on their way.

The Germans knew of the town mayor, Horace Tabor, who had staked many prospectors. They stood in front of his store a long time, wondering if they should go in.

"Ach, a stake to us he von't give," Hook said.

"But maybe vee shutt try."

Tabor, a 47-year-old Vermont native, had enjoyed modest success prospecting in the 1859 Colorado gold rush, but he preferred keeping store. He and his wife, Augusta, a distant relative of President Pierce, had followed the gold and silver booms from one mining camp to another. Augusta took in boarders, did laundry, and served as postmistress to help make ends meet.

A hard worker, Tabor was also coarse, brutish, and

elemental in both emotions and mental attitude. Some said he had no creases in either his trousers or his brains. Awkward and brusque, he made fun of the posturing that passed for gentility. He first kissed Augusta at their marriage ceremony. He offered no help as she raised their son, Maxcy. His wife constantly ridiculed Tabor for his lack of manners.

When Hook and Rische walked in, Tabor took his time sorting the mail and then walked over to them. Already learning the ingratiating gestures of the politician, he laid his hands on their shoulders.

"What kin I do for yuh, boys," he asked.

For the hundredth time he heard a plea for a grubstake from some seedy prospectors.

"Wal, pick out what yuh need. Yuh kin sign over a third of what yuh find. I'm always glad to help out."

The bill reached $64.75, including a jug of whiskey. Tabor wrote a note in his books, and all three signed. He didn't expect to hear any more from them.

Early the next morning, carrying new picks and shovels, the Germans climbed Fryer Hill and located their claim. Eight days later they had a shaft down twenty-nine feet. Their first ore brought eight hundred dollars a ton. They went directly to Tabor and handed him his share.

Hook named the mine the Little Pittsburgh in honor of his home town. By July they were shipping $10,000 worth of ore a week. They doubled that in August. By September, the money rolled in so fast it swept Hook off his feet. Afraid he was losing his mind and wanting to enjoy the money before it was lost, he sold his interest to Rische and Tabor for $98,000.

Hook bought a farm with his money, lived to a ripe old age, and died wealthy.

Two months later Rische felt dizzy as he watched his pile grow like Jack's bean stalk. He sold out for $262,000 to David H. Moffat, a friend of Tabor's from pioneer days in what had come to be called Denver.

"How do you want your money, Mister Rische?" asked Moffat's lawyer.

"All in tousant dollar bills, I vant."

The lawyer handed Rische a basket filled to the brim. Rische stayed in the Rockies, dabbling in mining. But drinking and gambling took his money. He saved enough to buy a saloon, but he eventually lost that. Moffat rescued Riche from the gutter with a job as watchman at the state capitol. Rische died old and broke.

Tabor, rich beyond dreams, was regarded as a demigod in Leadville. His good luck knew no end. One day he bought a claim from Chicken Bill Lovell for a thousand dollars. Chicken Bill had dug a twenty-foot shaft, finding nothing. Then he salted the bottom with ore stolen from the Little Pittsburgh. Tabor had been given a $500 check from Marshall Field of Chicago, before Field had become the merchandising king.

"Invest it if you find a good thing," Field had said.

Tabor considered the new claim half his and half Field's. Unconcerned when he learned the mine had been salted, Tabor told his men to dig deeper. At thirty feet they found an extensive vein of silver. A few months later, Tabor sold his interest for $500,000. Shortly after that, Field sold out for $700,000. The mine was then capitalized for ten million and lasted until 1927.

As Tabor bought and sold other mines, he continued running his store and handling Leadville's mail. He did give up his job as county treasurer, probably not wanting to mix his money with the county's.

One day a local pastor asked Tabor for a two hundred dollar donation so they could buy two chandeliers for the church.

"You sure two's enough?" Tabor asked, reaching into his pocket. "A church's gotta make a lot of noise to be heard in this place."

"'Twill be sufficient," Pastor Thomas Uzzell said.

"Well, I dunno." Tabor handed the money over. "By the way, Tom, who's gonna play them there chandeliers?"

Tabor equipped a fire department and built a city auditorium for Leadville. He built the Tabor Opera House, the largest building in the largest city in Colorado. He formed a small army of light cavalry to help patrol the streets. Unsuccessful in bringing the state capitol to Leadville, Tabor moved to Denver and dreamed bigger dreams. He served a term as lieutenant governor.

Tired of Augusta's prim, judgmental ways, Tabor took up with Baby Doe McCourt, a married woman from Wisconsin. She divorced her husband and began meeting Tabor secretly in Leadville and Denver.

In 1882 Tabor built the Tabor Grand Opera House, the largest theater in the United States. He sent his architects to Europe to study theaters in London, Paris, Vienna, and Berlin.

"But don't pattern if after them chicken coops," he said. "Jest pick up any ideas they left layin' around — anything we might use, git me?"

He also sent men to Belgium for carpets, France for tapestries, Japan for cherry logs, and Honduras for a mahogany forest to use in interior trim.

That fall the Colorado Legislature had two United States Senate terms to fill — thirty days to complete the term of Henry Teller, who had moved into President Arthur's cabinet, and a full six-year term. Rumors about Tabor's extra-marital adventures meant that he, the bankroller of the state Republican party, had to take the short term. But it was enough to complete the grandest dream of all. He would marry Baby Doe in Washington with the president an invited guest!

Tabor's one-month term in the Senate in January, 1893, was marked by one party after another. Baby Doe, a Catholic, wanted the ceremony performed by a priest. So Tabor concealed from the church that they had both been divorced.

When the ceremony ended, Tabor clapped President Arthur on the back.

"Well, Chester, did yuh have a good time? Wasn't the flowers purty? How 'bout a little snort on the side — jest me'n you?"

The astonished president stared as the 62-year-old bridegroom headed for the punch bowl. He smiled indulgently, refused the drink, and made a hasty exit.

Baby Doe had a daughter the following July. The proud parents named her Elizabeth Pearl. A second daughter, born in January, 1890, got her name from a lawyer, planning to run for the United States Congress that year. When Tabor led William Jennings Bryan up to the crib for a look, the baby laughed.

"Senator," Bryan said, "that baby's laughter has the ring of a silver dollar." Thus was Silver Dollar Tabor named.

Most persons would find it hard to throw away ten to fifteen million dollars, particularly if their income was a million a year. But with household expenses that included three carriages so Baby Doe could match colors to her dresses, and with investments in mines, hotels, and acreage across North America, Tabor did it.

Horace Tabor got appointed postmaster of Denver for an annual salary of $3500, a sum he had often won or lost on a single hand of poker. He did a good job, working faithfully in the building that had been constructed on land he had once owned and donated to the government. On April 10, 1899, he died of appendicitis. His funeral produced one of the largest civic turnouts in Colorado history.

Suggested reading: David Karsner, *Silver Dollar* (New York: Crown Publishers, 1953).

TOMBSTONE

Ed Schieffelin was under thirty when he came to Arizona Territory in 1877, but he looked much older. Old clothes, patched and re-patched with buckskin, hung in tatters on his six feet two frame. A gaunt scarecrow of a man, his dark curly hair hung below his shoulders. His blue eyes looked strange in his dark, sunburned face.

Ed had been prospecting in California, Nevada, Idaho, Colorado, and New Mexico, since leaving his Oregon home ten years before. His parents had emigrated to Oregon from Pennsylvania when Ed was nine. Ed was beginning to wonder if he just liked to see what was over the next ridge. Like all prospectors, he thought he wanted to strike it rich. But unlike most of them, he did not drink or gamble. Sometimes he had money; most of the time he didn't. It seemed to make no difference.

Ed had ridden down from Prescott with a cavalry troop who came to build a post in the Huachuca Mountains. The soldiers warned him about hostile Apaches. But Ed liked the looks of the country and decided to prospect it.

He rode his mule to a house built by a man named Brucknow, near present Fairbank in the San Pedro Valley. The occupants, taciturn, rough-appearing men, looked Ed over from hooded eyes but made no objection to his sleeping there while he searched the hills. They had seen other crazy prospectors risking their lives in futile searches. They said nothing about themselves and asked no questions. It was soon clear to Ed that the house was a rendezvous for Mexican smugglers, but it was also a place where he could sleep in safety from Apaches.

One day one of the occupants asked him a question. "What for do you-all take them pasears out in the hot desert every day?"

"Just looking for rocks."

"Well, all I got to say is that what you find will be your own tombstone."

One night Ed came close. That day he had found where two prospectors had been killed by Apaches a few months before. Someone had buried the men, but not the specimens of rock they had carried. Ed recognized the silver in the specimens and he followed up a dry wash that led away from the graves. From time to time he picked up more rocks, the float that had worked its way down over the centuries from

ED SCHIEFFELIN

Arizona Historical Society

the lode, somewhere up ahead. From time to time he dismounted from his mule and crept to the ridge on one side or the other to look for Apaches.

The day wore on as Ed climbed upward under the hot sun, stopping now to examine and keep another rock, now to crawl to the ridge and watch for Apaches. Finally he realized that the afternoon shadows had covered the land, leaving only the high peaks in the sunshine. Then he picked up a blackish rock. Horn silver! Ed recognized it from his days of prospecting the Comstock in Nevada. He looked around for more, excited at the most promising find he had ever made.

His enthusiasm vanished when he noticed that darkness was falling rapidly. It was too late to get back to the safety of the Bruncknow house. He would have to camp out in the hostile land!

Ed led his mule into the hills and picketed it where passing Apaches would not see it. Then he found his own hiding place a mile away, where three huge knolls of granite boulders rose beside the wash. He crawled to the highest, determined to keep watch all night if he could stay awake.

But when Ed peeked over the top of a boulder, he dropped as if he had been shot. An Apache, his taut body leaning forward, his rifle across his thighs, was riding up to the knoll. While Ed had climbed one slope, the Indian had started up the other to look for enemies. Surely others would be close by!

Ed peeped out a narrow crack between two boulders and saw another Indian on the summit of the next knoll. Afoot, this Indian was searching the landscape for any sign of movement. He was so near that Ed saw the war paint on his ugly face. Ed crooked his thumb over the hammer of his rifle and slowly eased it to full cock. The first Apache had dismounted and was climbing the rock below Ed. Then Ed heard the clink of horses' hooves and saw at least thirty more savages moving up the trail.

Ed's mind went to that comment at the Brucknow house: "You-all will sure find your tombstone out there." He thought of what the two prospectors at the mouth of the wash must have felt — that fate had dealt a losing hand.

Then one of the sentinels signaled the other, and they both started down the knolls, toward the other Indians. The rattle of hooves grew fainter. Ed lowered the hammer of his rifle and took his first deep breath.

But he did not dare leave. He might wander into another place where the Indians would find him without shelter. So he waited for sunrise and the beginning of the attack.

When the color came back to the east, he saw no sign of creeping savages. The sun rose and still nothing moved. He made his way back to the Brucknow house.

Ed was almost out of provisions. He would have to get a grubstake before he could continue his search for the outcropping vein. His brother, Al, was working at a mine in Mohave County. He and a friend, Dick Gird, a part-time assayer, looked at the specimens and agreed to become Ed's partners. It was spring 1878 before the three of them returned to the dry wash and staked their claims. They made the Brucknow house their headquarters even though it had two more fresh graves by its adobe walls.

But when they dug down three feet, the vein they found pinched out. The claims had not been worth staking!

After a conference, the partners decided to look for another vein in the same general area, even though the Apaches were back on the warpath. One morning after a night in the hills, they found an Apache wristlet in the bear-grass a hundred yards from where they had been sleeping. But that same day, Ed found a new outcropping, a big strike. He called it the Tombstone and explained to his partners about the prediction of the man at the Bruncknow house.

Ed and his partners became wealthy from the Tombstone silver mines. But Ed was cut out to be a prospector, not a wealthy miner. Although he had more money than he could ever spend, he thought that a giant circle of gold and silver ore ran from Asia to Cape Horn, crossing the Bering Strait to the Rocky Mountains and on down through North America to the Andes in South America.

He searched for ore in South America with little success. His last prospecting trip was at the Yukon River in Alaska. He found gold all along the river, but the old prospector, used to the blazing Arizona sun, did not like the bleak arctic summer. He gave up shortly before reaching the Klondike River. He returned to his Oregon cabin, where he died of a heart attack in 1897, a few months after gold was discovered on the Klondike.

Ed's friends followed his directions and buried him on the knoll where he had spent the night among the Apaches. The town of Tombstone lies three miles east.

Suggested reading: Frederick R. Bechdolt, *When the West was Young* (New York: The Century Co., 1922).

Tommy Cruse

Tommy Cruse had always been late. When the twenty-year-old Irishman reached New York in 1856, the only jobs for immigrants from the Emerald Isle were hard and dirty. He struggled for seven years and then went west to prospect for gold. But 1863 and 1864 were hard years in California and Nevada. Tommy still lived on cabbage and beans, eaten after long, bone-aching days of toil.

In 1865 he went to Alder Gulch, Montana. He told his friends: "Shure and perhaps the good lord will smile on me at last. It's many pans I've washed out for nothing but experience."

But Alder Gulch was covered with located claims, with no place for a newcomer. Too late again.

The Salmon River mines over in Idaho were no better. Tommy returned to Montana in 1867, this time to Helena.

But Last Chance Gulch, where a man could accidentally find enough gold while digging the foundation to pay for his building, had no room for Tommy. He struggled through nine winters, setting out each spring with pan, shovel, and high hopes. Bankers, asked for grubstakes, looked at the stooped, man, aged beyond his years, and shook their heads.

Then in April, 1876, Tommy worked his lonely way up Silver Creek, twenty-two miles north of Helena. He found smooth gold quartz "float" in the stream bed. It turned rougher and richer and then disappeared completely.

In thirteen years prospecting Tommy had learned that float quartz usually came from the erosion of a mother lode, and the rougher it was, the closer it was to its starting point. His heart raced as he left the stream bed, moved into the timber and started digging. Suddenly he found it — a foot-wide vein of gold-filled rock.

Tommy staked his claim and guarded it until dark. That night he traveled back to Helena to register the claim, the largest gold-quartz vein in Montana history. He called it the Drum Lemmon after his native parish in County Cavan, Ireland.

Suddenly Tommy was *Mister* Cruse. No longer did he face patronizing smiles or hear "crazy old man" snickers behind his back. In four years he took out a million dollars. Then he sold out for another million and one-third of future profits.

Tommy formed his own bank to handle his money. He married Margaret Carter, the sister of a prominent local politician. And what a wedding that was! Sixteen hundred quarts of champagne, brought in from Chicago, kept Helena afloat from dawn to midnight of the wedding day. No one could buy a drink! All the saloons and all the water coolers in the hotels dispensed Tommy's champagne. Men rode into Helena from a hundred miles to see Tommy, resplendent in his Prince Albert coat, white gloves and tie, and to drink his champagne.

Ten months later, fifty-year-old Tommy became a proud father and a grieving widower on the same day. Margaret died delivering the baby, Mary Margaret. The doll-like girl became Tommy's new passion, replacing the old one of finding gold. He called her Mamie, and the town called him Colonel.

As Colonel Cruse did his bank business, little Mamie played on the floor by his huge, roll-top desk. She learned to clog dance on bars, nodding at the smiles and hand clapping of gentlemen watchers.

"A little sweet refreshment for the sweet little lady?" the bartender would ask.

"Just a wee drop of the green," said the proud colonel.

When Mamie was seven, the panic of 1893 ruined many banks, but not her father's. Other banks came to him for loans. Remembering their rejections from years before, Colonel Cruse said; "Shure yez can get a loan — it's four percent a month it is, and then only as an accommodation fer ye."

Maybe it was the taste of the crème de menthe, or maybe it would have happened anyway. Tommy never heard the rumors, but the town was full of them as Mamie grew up — rumors of drugs and alcohol. She died at twenty-seven, after what the papers called "many years of failing health." By then Tommy had pledged a quarter of a million dollars to the building of a Roman Catholic cathedral in Helena, the grandest building between the Twin Cities and the Pacific Coast. Its completion became his new passion. He cared very little for living things after Mamie's death.

Tommy died one week after the cathedral dedication. At that dedication, some had noticed that Tommy held his prayer book upside down. He had never learned to read or write.

Suggested reading: John K. Hutchens, *One Man's Montana* (Philadelphia: J. B. Lippincott Company, 1964).

BEARTOWN

Beartown, Montana left a colorful history. Thirty miles east of Missoula and once a contender for state capital, it produced over a million dollars in gold and silver in 1866 and 1867.

The pay streak in Bear and Deep Gulches was rich and narrow. The four-block town, its buildings jammed up against a hill, contained a hotel, a general store, a brewery, several blacksmith shops, a jail, and seventeen saloons. The general store was owned and operated by a Frenchman and a Spaniard, neither of whom could understand the other.

At first there were no law officers. Then the miners discovered that an Irishman named McElroy knew legal terms and was fluent with them when drunk, although tounge-tied when sober. They elected him justice of the peace and kept him well oiled.

Beartown's miners settled arguments on its famous Fighting Bar. When Mike Kelly jumped the claim of a Chinese miner, and the owner protested, they shot it out on the bar. The Chinese shot Mike in the face. Mike claimed that he had been shot with his own bullet, ricocheting off the bullet of his opponent.

Old Greenwood was one of the good-natured characters of Beartown. Mining alone, he would shovel gravel into the ore bucket at the bottom of his deep shaft.

"Hoist away, up there," he would shout to his non-existent partner.

After waiting a reasonable time, he would climb to the surface, and hoist the load himself, all the time cursing his absent helper.

Doctor Armistead Mitchell, a Deer Lodge surgeon, made rounds in the mining camps. Once he reached Beartown shortly after a miner named Shorty had fallen into his own fireplace while drunk, roasting his arm to a crisp. With a plank across two barrels for an operating table, the doctor loaded his patient up with whiskey, took some himself, and amputated the arm. He saved the charred flesh and bone fragments in a sack for further study. He played poker the rest of the afternoon and was guest of honor at a dance that evening, put on by the local madam with her girls and attended by all the men of Beartown.

When the party broke up, the doctor started down the trail, singing lustily and waving the sack with Shorty's arm. But somewhere along the trail he lost his prized medical specimen!

Holidays were important to the miners. Someone read the Declaration of Independence every Fourth of July. At Christmas, when the snow was too deep to work their claims, the miners went to Helena, Missoula, or Deer Lodge for benders. Extra supplies of liquor were always laid in for September 5th, Miners Union Day.

Funerals were also important. Bear Gulch was so narrow that only seven bodies were buried there. The rest were packed out by mules to Deer Lodge. The mourners followed, singing sad songs to show respect for the dead and dance hall songs as a celebration for the living.

Mike Flynn, who died during the 1870 winter, had been promised a Christian burial in consecrated ground by his partner. Mike's friends packed him out to the mouth of the gulch and then knocked together a crude coffin. They borrowed a wagon and a team to carry Mike the rest of the way.

They reached Pioneer Bar by late afternoon and stopped for a drink. One called for another, and, since Mike, a good Irishman, had not yet had his wake, they stayed all night and did it up right. They sat the coffin on two beer kegs, lit some candles, and enjoyed a full night of singing and drinking.

By morning most of the boys were not fit to travel, so two of them rode on to Deer Lodge to see the priest and dig the grave. It was almost dark when the wagon and the rest of Mike's friends arrived. But the coffin was not in the wagon! It had slipped out someplace back on the trail.

At the priest's suggestion, the mourners spent the night in Deer Lodge and hunted for Mike in the morning. They found the coffin standing on one end in a creek bed. They drained the water out, brought Mike on in, and gave him the promised Christian burial.

Suggested reading: Muriel S. Wolle, *Montana Pay Dirt* (Denver: Sage Books, 1963).

HUMAN MOLE

Canadian Elie Ritchott was working a claim in the Quartz Creek Mining District of Mineral County, Montana Territory, in 1880. He had sunk a four feet by six feet shaft down to bedrock, forty-two feet below the surface, where he found a buried gravel bar from an ancient stream bed. He had tunneled two hundred feet along the top of the bedrock, removing gravel as he went. The gravel was rich in gold and worth bringing to the surface, where Elie washed it out in his sluice boxes. But it was mighty hard work.

Here is what Elie, working alone, had to do each weary day: He climbed down the wooden ladder which he had built in the shaft. Then he crawled to the end of the tunnel to continue digging. The tunnel was four feet wide. Since the gold lay close to bedrock, Elie kept the tunnel roof as low as possible to avoid removing any more earth than necessary. The roof was less than five feet high.

When Elie had filled his bucket, he wheeled it to the shaft on a track that he had laid in the bottom of the tunnel. He hooked a windlass rope to the bucket and climbed the ladder to the surface. Then he wound the windlass to raise the bucket. He dumped the bucket into a car which ran on a surface track. He pushed the car to his sluice boxes, emptied it, and washed the gravel to recover his gold. Then he pushed the car back to the top of the shaft, lowered the bucket with the windlass, and went back down the ladder to fill the bucket again. As he worked at the end of his tunnel, he looked forward to returning again to the surface where he could stand erect and breathe fresh air.

Elie had timbered the shaft and the tunnel to keep them from caving in. But one morning, just as he was starting to dig at the end of the tunnel, Elie heard a dreaded rumble behind him, and he knew his tunnel was collapsing. When the horrible noise stopped, Elie felt relief to be alive. But when he crawled back about sixty feet he found the tunnel filled solid.

Elie's nearest neighbor was a half mile away. It could be days before anyone discovered what had happened. He knew he could not live that long without fresh air. He decided to dig as long as he could. Trying to escape was better that sitting helpless, waiting for death to come. He had three candles, which he thought would last from fifteen to eighteen hours.

Afraid that the tunnel was filled in all the way back to the shaft, Elie decided to angle upward toward the surface, which he calculated was thirty-eight feet above him.

After digging fourteen hours he broke through into a chamber left by the cave-in. He realized, by the size and direction of the chamber, that the closest way out was to dig back down to the part of the tunnel beyond that which had collapsed.

He had three inches of his last candle left. It provided light for two more feet of digging. He worked in total darkness after that.

Elie kept his crowbar with him to loosen the earth and rocks. He painfully scraped the loosened material back to his feet as he slowly wormed ahead. Always afraid of another cave-in, he kept the hole as small as possible.

Finally he felt the crowbar strike the timbering at the top of the tunnel. He worked a long time in his cramped position before he could pry the timbers enough to smell the fresh air.

Elie realized then that he had been dazed or semi-conscious for some unknown length of time. Breathing the fresh air revived him, and he could think clearly again.

Later he would describe the air to friends: "Better than anything to eat; better than anything to drink; better than anything in the world. And I knew then that I was going to get out."

It still took him several hours to break enough timbering that he could squeeze down into the tunnel. By the time he got through, the loose earth from his digging had almost filled the tunnel just below.

Elie rested for a few minutes and than crawled out to the shaft. He looked hungrily at the blue sky, which he had thought he would never see again.

It took a long time in his weakness to climb the ladder. He rested at the surface and then struggled to his cabin. The sun told him that it was evening, but it seemed that he had been underground longer than one day.

When he saw the clock he realized that he had been digging for 35 1/2 hours. He made a cup of coffee and crawled into bed. He slept until noon the next day.

Elie worked the claim for two more years.

"But I never went back into that tunnel," he said. "I sure had enough of it."

Suggested reading: Jean Davis, *Shallow Diggin's* (Caldwell: The Caxton Printers, 1963).

BULLS, BEARS, DOGS AND WILDCATS

Underground miners led tough lives in brutal places. Their entertainment sometimes matched their working conditions. Two animal fights in Virginia City, Nevada, in 1871 provide good examples.

Both fights were staged in the Piper Opera House. The first, held Sunday, August 6, pitted a bull against a bear. The theater was already crowded two hours before the fight began. At 8:20 the gate into the wire cage at the center of the arena slid up, and the bear walked in leisurely. A large brown bear from California's Coast Range, he sniffed at the bars of the cage and then took up a stand at the opposite gate where the bull would enter. The crowd cheered hoarsely.

"He smells the bull," someone shouted.

"Who says he won't fight?. He can't wait to get at the bull!"

They had to wait until the bear moved away before they could open the bull's gate. By the time the bull stalked in, the bear was cowering across the cage. The heavily muscled, "fierce-looking" animal shook his head and charged the bear. The bear roared as the bull gouged with his horns. The bear clawed the bull about the head and escaped.

Another charge, the bear's desperate defense with teeth and claws, and a third charge brought the animals to a stand-off. The bull pawed the ground for ten minutes before charging again. He jammed the bear against the cage, but the bear clawed and roared and slunk away to another corner.

The miners could see the bear's fright and the bull's reluctance to continue. Some of them crawled up on the roof of the cage and poured blood down on the bull, who pawed slowly, his eyes glaring at his adversary. Others fastened a red cloth to a pole and waved it back and forth near the bear.

But both animals stubbornly kept the peace. The miners drove the bear out of his corner at the rear of the cage. He moved to the front and laid down. Again they poked at him with whips and iron bars, but he only got mad at the miners, roaring and striking at them.

Responding to cries of "Stir up the bull," others on top of the cage prodded the animal with long poles. Instead of charging the bear, the bull crashed against the bars, shaking and rattling the entire cage. Two bars bent apart, and a large gap showed. Nearby spectators fled in panic.

Someone fired a rifle at the bull. The bullet split on a bar, and a piece of it hit a spectator, who also held a rifle in his hands. He was not seriously injured, but his yell that he had been hit added to the excitement.

Now the miners left the bull alone and confined their stirring-up to the bear, who stood it well. When the bear refused to get to his feet, the show's promoter stepped forward.

"The bull wins," he announced. "The bear's nearly dead."

Angry hooting followed. "The fight must go on!"

The gas was turned off, and many spectators left. But the majority remained, barely able to make out the cage and the animals in the dim light. Then the spectators took over.

They threw chairs against the cage. Over a hundred of them rushed the cage, shaking the bars and trying to stir the tired animals into more fight. The few remaining lights went out, and the miners struck matches, demanding that the lights go back on.   The promoter turned the lights back on and came down to the cage amid hissing and hooting.

"I've done all I can to make them fight," he insisted. "If you can do better, name a committee and go to it.   I'll provide the gas if you want to go all night."

A volunteer committee took control, making an immediate plea for firecrackers. A large package landed on the stage. As a miner opened the firecrackers and was about to strike a match, the theater's property manager pointed out that too many firecrackers might set the theater on fire.

Bayonets and knives were then mounted on poles and used to prod the animals. Finally, convinced that the bear would no longer fight, the miners reluctantly abandoned the theater.

The newspaper finished its report:

"Our people have now seen a bull and bear fight, and we venture to say that they will never care to see another — prodding the animals to make them fight is a cruel business."

The next fight was staged six weeks later. Two wildcats, captured near Dayton, were matched against a local rancher's bulldog, Hero. Five hundred dollars in coin was bet on the wildcats against ten oxen, put up by the rancher, Mr. Gee. A ten foot by twelve foot cage of iron bars, ten feet high, with a back and roof of boards was the place of combat. Gas jets lighted the cage interior so all spectators could see.

The female of the wildcat pair was thrown in first. Hero,

an intelligent, white bulldog, soon followed. The cat rushed wildly in all directions, trying frantically to get away. Within a minute of his entry into the cage, Hero had grabbed her by the neck and shaken her to death.

Hero was sponged off and treated like an old prizefighter. Spectators cheered. Those who had bet on the dog waited expectantly. After a short pause, the male wildcat was put in and Hero went after him. Spectators hooted that this would be another quick killing.

But this cat met Hero with two gouging digs from sharp claws into the nose. Hero dodged and barked and jumped about and finally retreated, "docile, badly winded, and demoralized." Gee took him out for a drink and a short rest and put him back in for a second round.

After another furious beating, Hero retired to the bars in disgrace. Gee let him out and announced that he had given up his part of the bet. He would keep the oxen and make no claim on the coin.

Some spectators, unhappy that all bets were not resolved, raised money to buy the wildcat and match him against a little black bulldog belonging to James Kelly. After new bets had been made, the dog, no bigger than his adversary, was put into the cage with the wildcat. Unafraid of claws or teeth, the dog got a grip on the cat's neck and held on like a vice. The cat fought well, scratching and biting, but after twenty minutes he lay dead. The little dog was taken away amid enthusiastic cheers from his supporters.

Suggested reading: *Virginia City Territorial Enterprise,* Aug. 6, 1871; *Gold Hill Daily News,* Sept. 23, 1871.

SMALL BLUE PEBBLES

Sixteen-year-old Jake Hoover came to the Judith Basin of Montana in the early 1870s to start a cattle ranch. He settled on the South Fork of the Judith River and prospected for gold when he had the time. He had good luck prospecting. He was in the gold rush to Yogo Creek in 1879, and he became the first recorder for the mining district. Hoover City, one of two mining camps in Yogo Gulch, was named for him.

In 1894 Jake and Frank Hobson, prospecting in the Little Belt Mountains, took refuge under a rocky ledge during a mountain storm. They saw flakes of gold in a crevice. Development was slow, as water had to be ditched in from Yogo Creek at a cost of 38,000 dollars. It was also unprofitable, as only a thousand dollars in gold was recovered.

But whenever they cleaned out their sluice boxes, they noticed small blue pebbles caught in the riffles with the gold. They threw the pebbles out with the rest of the trash.

After the gold mining stopped, Hobson went to Maine to visit. There he told a school teacher friend about his mining experiences. He agreed to send her some specimens of gold ore which she could show to her pupils.

When he got home, Hobson packed up some dust, along with a few of the blue pebbles, and sent them to the teacher. In her thank you letter, the teacher said nothing about the gold, but thanked Hobson for the sapphires, which she had had appraised.

What the hell is a sapphire? Hobson wondered. A jeweler in Helena told him they were gem stones, and very good ones.

But Jake's wife, a bad-tempered woman, was causing him trouble. She often threatened to kill him, and she had shot at him twice. So Jake sold out and moved to Alaska. His wife, trying to follow, lost the trail. Later she married another rancher, who killed her in self defense.

Montana sapphires are the only ones mined in the western hemisphere. High in quality, they are usually free from flaws. Between twenty and thirty million dollars worth of sapphires have come out of Montana. Of course they did Jake Hoover little good.

Suggested reading: Muriel S. Wolle, *Montana Pay Dirt* (Denver: Sage Books, 1963).

PRUNES

When Rupert Sherwood started prospecting in the Fairplay-Alma area of Colorado's South Park in 1877 he quickly got a new friend. Prunes, who would become Colorado's most famous burro, had been considered a community animal, ready to serve any prospector who fed him and gave him a job. Rupe had plenty for Prunes to do, and he fed the burro well. The pair were inseparable for many decades.

Rupe liked placer mining along stream beds. Traveling from one prospect to another, Prunes carried his equipment, blankets, cooking pots, and food, in addition to oats for himself. Rupe would tie a rope from Prunes' packsaddle to his pick and use the little animal to plow up the hard ground. Then Rupe would shovel the loosened earth on to a rough-built sled and have Prunes drag it down to running water so Rupe could wash out the gold.

Sometimes Rupe tired of panning. If timber was available for building sluice boxes, Rupe would cut the trees, and his faithful burro would haul the logs down to the stream.

When Rupe did not find enough gold to keep prospecting for himself, he and Prunes worked at hard rock mining for others. Then the little burro would winch the ore to the surface and carry it to the mill. Rupe made a good living in the mines, but he never got rich, so Prunes became famous for having worked in almost every hard rock mine in South Park.

When Rupe got old he started spending his winters in Denver, leaving Prunes in Fairplay. The town residents lovingly provided hay, biscuits, and pancakes, as Prunes made the rounds for his handouts. Rupe would return each spring to a hearty "mountain canary" welcome from his old friend.

Rupe's friends gave him an eightieth birthday party. They included a bag of oats for his partner. Prunes, almost blind and toothless, could hardly eat his treat.

The next winter Fairplay children found Prunes near death after a severe blizzard. Their mothers kept the burro alive until Rupe returned in spring 1930. Then the townspeople convinced Rupe that the kindest thing to do was to shoot his old partner.

Rupe had Prunes buried beside one of Fairplay's streets. Within a year the old man was dead. At his request, his ashes were buried next to Prunes.

Suggested reading: Myriam Friggens, *Tales, Trails and Tommyknockers* (Boulder: Johnson Books, 1979).

PRUNES and FRIENDS

MINERS' COURT

A deep, narrow gulch in the heart of the Taos Range of New Mexico was first prospected by four or five men from Tennessee. They found gold, but unearthly moans and screams at night drove them away. They called it Whooping Hollow, and they wanted no more of it. The strange sounds seemed to come from a haunt or ghost, high above on the ridge.

Other prospectors moved in. They decided the mournful sounds came from a screech owl, and they stayed. The town that grew in the bottom of the gorge had five stores and thirty saloons. One thing that Whooping Hollow never had was a church service. Now and then a fight at a gambling table would end up with another miner taking up his last claim — six feet by two — in the bone orchard. But the miners were no more lawless than most.

Lemuel Knaggs, an old timer who had been in on the California, British Columbia, and Pike's Peak gold rushes, was the town's leading citizen. He always wore a navy shirt with a curious collar button. Under the watchful care of Knaggs and a few others, Whooping Hollow prospered for two or three years. Then a pall suddenly fell. Men began disappearing. A man would announce that he was going to visit a neighboring camp or take a hunting trip, and he would never be seen again.

Someone noticed that the men who disappeared all had said they were going in the direction of Sandy Bar. Only one trail left Whooping Hollow in that direction. It went through a narrow, rocky valley called Willow Springs Gulch.

Willow Springs Gulch had long since been mined out. Only one man still lived in the dreary place. No one knew his true name. He was a rough, illiterate giant called Willow Springs Jack. His only redeeming quality was his kindness to his dog, Jupe. Jupe was a mangy, one-eyed, tailless cur, a fitting partner for his master.

One day, Lemuel Knaggs said he was going over to Sandy Bar. He was never seen again. With Whooping Hollow's leading citizen missing, lynch talk started about Willow Springs Jack. But before the miners went after Jack, their culprit came to them.

Jack said he knew he was suspected. He could not understand why none of the men who disappeared had ever got as far as his cabin. So he had begun his own detective work. The only cabin on the Sandy Bar trail between him and Whooping Hollow was Ike Plodgett's. He knew Plodgett had gone hunting, so he searched the trail around Plodgett's cabin. There, Jupe dug up a human foot. Near the foot was an unusual button. Jack brought the button to town. Knaggs' friends recognized it.

"This man's either telling the truth or he's the murderer hisself," said one of the miners.

Ike Plodgett was one of the Hollow's best miners. He had a fine, paying claim, and he worked it hard. Sure, he drank and gambled, but who didn't? The other miners decided to look around before Plodgett returned from his hunting trip. They found Knaggs' body buried near the trail. They found many more bodies, buried under the floor of Plodgett's cabin. They knew Plodgett would come through Whooping Hollow on his way home, so they went back to wait. They appointed Willow Springs Jack to make the arrest.

When Plodgett stepped down from his mule, Jack grabbed him. They convened the court quickly. Old Sam Bartlett, as usual, was the judge. Tom Bradford, as usual, was prosecutor. Enoch Green, a recent graduate of Yale Law School, was assigned to defend the accused.

The judge summarized the evidence. A deathlike stillness fell over the crowd as the judge reviewed the evidence found at Plodgett's cabin. Revolvers began to click. Some wondered if the proceedings would end before the prosecutor and defense lawyer had their chances to speak.

Bradford reiterated some of what the judge had so forcefully said. Then young Enoch Green had his turn. He made an eloquent appeal, and the crowd looked at him with menacing glances. The judge held up his hand, made another address, and charged the jury to return their verdict.

The twelve men put their heads together, without leaving their seats. They all stood, faced the judge, and shouted, "Guilty!"

Two burly miners took Plodgett to the nearest tree. It was just after midnight. When the sun rose the next morning, Plodgett's lifeless body was still twisting slowly above the main street of Whooping Hollow.

Suggested reading: Henry Inman, *Tales of the Trail* (Topeka: Crane & Co., 1898).

TERMINATION OF PARTNERSHIP

In May 1886 three prospectors in Butte City, Montana Territory, decided to try their luck in the Jackson Hole country, further south.   All Germans, they decided at the last minute to take in another partner, John Tonnar, also an immigrant from Germany.

On the way down they stopped in Idaho Territory to visit Emile Wolff. Wolff had come to the United States from Germany at sixteen to join the army. When his enlistment expired at Fort Hall, he had started ranching in the Teton Valley, near where trappers had fought Indians at the famous Battle of Pierre's Hole. Wolff had been a schoolmate in Luxembourg of Henry Welter, one of the prospectors.

Welter introduced Wolff to his other partners, August Kellenberger, T. H. Tigerman, and Tonnar. The miners left some supplies at Wolff's ranch and crossed the Teton Pass into Jackson Hole, where they planned to prospect on the Snake River.

A few days later, Tonnar and Kellenberger returned to pick up the supplies they had left behind. They said they were prospecting right in the middle of Jackson Hole. Wolff heard no more about them until July 19, when Tonnar showed up.

Tonnar said his three partners had gone hunting and he was lonesome, so he came over the pass for a visit.   But Tonnar acted strange. He said nothing, as the days went on, about returning to his partners. Wolff didn't ask questions, as it was haying season and he needed an extra man.

But Wolff noticed that Tonnar always had a gun within reach. Then one day the man showed Wolff where he had hidden a silver watch and a purse containing twenty-eight dollars.

"The watch and money you haff, Emile, if to me something happen," Tonnar said, smiling.

Wolff's rising suspicions were answered one day when the sheriff from Wyoming Territory rode over the pass, asking if he had seen Tonnar.

"He's wanted for murder," the sheriff said. "He butchered his three partners."

Remembering the ever-present gun and that they had slept by the same fire for a few weeks, Wolff gasped, "My God! He's out in the hayfield. Grab him while you can."

After the arrest, the sheriff told Wolff that Frank Free

from Ione, California, had been hunting and fishing in the Tetons with friends. One day he saw what looked like a suddenly-deserted mining camp on the north bank of the Snake, due east of the south shore of Jenny Lake, where the river runs almost straight west. Following the river downstream he found a low pile of rocks with some clothing and a human hand visible. The rest of the grisly details soon came clear.

The head of Tiggerman, a giant of a man and the leader of the party, had been crushed by an axe. Kellenberger had been shot twice in the back, and Welter had been struck in the head with an axe.

"He must have killed them in their sleep," the sheriff said. "Looks like he rolled them into the river and covered them with rocks. If the river hadn't been dropping the last few days, the guy from California wouldn't have seen them. We asked around and found out there were four men altogether and they had come from this way. That's why I came up for a look."

By the time the trial started the next April down in Evanston, the watch and purse had been identified as belonging to Tiggerman.

Tonnar testified that the four partners had argued about building a dam to collect enough water to run their sluice box. During the argument, Tiggerman had hit him and held him under water until Tonnar almost drowned. Nothing more was said until the next morning, when, Tonnar claimed, they kicked him out as a partner. When Welter put on Tonnar's boots, Tonnar objected. Then they called him a son of a bitch and said they would kill him. Tiggerman had a shovel raised to strike, and Kellenberger was advancing with an axe when Tonnar ran for his gun and started shooting.

Tonnar, aged forty, was a small man, about a hundred forty pounds. He never explained the axe wounds or why he had stolen Tiggerman's watch and purse. The jury acquitted him on grounds of self defense.

Tonnar, apparently fearing vengeance from the victims' friends, moved back to Germany immediately. The scene of the crime has been called Deadman's Bar ever since.

Suggested reading: "The Story of Deadman's Bar," in *Annals of Wyoming, v. 5, pt. 4* (June, 1929).

LOST BREYFOGLE MINE

When news of a new silver strike in the Reese River District of Nevada reached Los Angeles in 1864, Jacob Breyfogle picked up his ears. He had been prospecting in Nevada for several years, using blacksmith work to earn his grub. Breyfogle, a big German with oversized feet, left immediately for Nevada with two companions, an Irishman named O'Bannion, and a Scotsman named McLeod. They took a direct path north, through some of the world's most inhospitable country. The fathers at the San Fernando Mission begged them in vain to give up their perilous trip.

The three prospectors crossed the Mohave Desert, skirted the Argus Range, struggled across the glittering waste of Panamint Valley and climbed into the dreadful Panamint Mountains. From the summit of the mountains they saw the unearthly basin of horrors called Death Valley and on beyond that the Funeral Range.

They followed an old Indian trail down from the summit. When they reached a spring, they stopped for the night. It was hard to find smooth places to lie on, so O'Bannion and McLeod slept together by the spring and Breyfogle moved two hundred yards down the slope. Following their custom, they slept in their clothing, removing only their shoes.

The screams and groans of his companions, being murdered by Indians, woke Breyfogle. He grabbed his shoes and ran toward the valley below. By daylight he had reached the floor of Death Valley. Fearful that the Indians would follow his bloody footprints over the rocks, the German hid for several hours. His feet were so bruised and ripped that he could not put on his shoes.

It was just as well. The blistering June sun beat down on his bare head. While crossing the ten-mile wide valley, he stumbled upon a little hole of alkali water, the first he had seen since the evening before. He felt deathly sick when he drank his fill, but he soon recovered. He filled his big shoes with water, and, carrying them as canteens, limped on.

After traveling about an hour into the foothills of the Funeral Range, he stopped and slept. He drank one shoeful during the night, the other at dawn. Sick again from the alkali, he started for the top of the range, about eight or ten miles ahead. About half way up the mountain, he saw a green spot about three miles to the south. He turned that way and had traveled about half the distance when he saw some grayish-white float rock with free gold showing all through it. He soon found the vein, a pinkish feldspar, even richer in gold.

Although he was still crazed with fear of the Indians and desperate for fresh water, Breyfogle stopped to fill his bandana with samples from the vein.

The green spot was a low mesquite bush with no water. He filled up on mesquite beans and collapsed. He lost his mind, but not his sense of direction. The next several days stayed forever a blank for him. But he kept moving north, across the Funeral Range and the Amargosa Desert. When he reached the fresh water of Baxter Springs, two hundred and fifty miles from where he had left Death Valley, he rested and recovered his mind. He must have had something to eat and drink during that travel, but he never remembered it.

A Rancher in Smoky Valley saw Breyfogle's oversized footprints and tracked him down. The huge man, almost naked, looked like a cadaverous giant from the searing fires of hell. His bald head had blistered down to the skull, and he looked scalped. He still carried his shoes, one of them filled with the ore samples.

The ore was half gold, assaying two thousand dollars a ton. Three months later, when it was cool enough for an expedition, Breyfogle and a half dozen others set out to find the vein. A war party of Panamint Indians turned them back. During the winter a dozen men tried again. Breyfogle found the alkali water hole where he had filled his shoes. He found the place where he had spent the night after his companions were murdered. He found what he thought was the mesquite bush, where his memory had gone blank. The area around it was no longer green.

"We must have passed it, a mile or two north of here," he said. "I remember finding the vein on my way down to the green place."

But there were other mesquite bushes. Breyfogle's companions searched frantically in every direction. Some jeered him; some cursed him for the wild goose chase. George Hearst, who later owned the largest gold mine in the world, kept his prospectors busy for two winters trying to find the vein. Some who've searched have never returned. Some search still. Many thought a cloudburst had covered the outcrop. Some hope that a new cloudburst will uncover it.

The gold is still there.

Suggested reading: J. Frank Dobie, *Coronado's Children* (New York: Grosset & Dunlap, 1930).

HIGH-GRADING IN GOLDFIELD

Some lode-mining districts produced gold ore so rich that it assayed from five dollars to over one hundred dollars a pound. Miners, blasting such ore out of deep and dangerous holes for $4.50 per day, recognized their opportunities. The mine operators, usually companies which had limited-term leases from the owners, could see the heavy lunch buckets and bulging pockets as the men went off shift. But they needed miners to get the ore out quickly, before the lease ran out. Besides, what they had left to sell still often brought a hundred thousand dollars a day.

Often the lessee-operators cheated the lessors. If the mine was incorporated, the lessors probably cheated the stockholders. So an orgy of high-grading (fancy term for stealing) passed up the line as each level cheated the one above. The operators did some inspecting to keep the stealing down to reasonable levels, and the miners countered with their own measures. Goldfield, Nevada, provides a good example, although Cripple Creek and Creede, both in Colorado, had the same problem. One report claimed that a million and a half was stolen from one Goldfield mine, the Jumbo, in 1904 alone. The miners did not think they were thieves. Working with such rich ores all day, they thought they were entitled to a little dividend.

Gold was first discovered in Goldfield in 1903. Results were modest, but the camp soon slumped. They had sunk their shafts in rock unlike any seen before, and three hundred tons of ore were dumped as worthless. Then J. P. Loftus, an Amherst graduate, picked up a rock that had been marked by the hobnails of a hundred passing boots. It assayed at fifty thousand dollars a ton. Goldfield came back with a rush.

Within three years the number of assayers had increased from one to sixty. Most of them bought ore from wage-earning miners, no questions asked, at about half its true value.

The miners disdained to hide anything worth only a dollar a pound. "Company ore," they would say, shoveling it into the ore buckets to be hoisted to the surface.

Miners who started out using lunch buckets and pockets to conceal the rich ore soon began wearing two shirts, sewed together at the bottom. When that approach became too bulky and awkward, they made special canvas jackets, with pockets extending from shoulder to bottom hem, so they could carry more ore with less bulges. Called corset covers, these jackets were soon being sold in the local stores.

Many mine operators and brokerage houses winked at high-grading. They thought the booming prosperity and wild life that came with it was good advertising for Goldfield and its mines. Arrests were made and some ore recovered, but that, too, was considered good publicity.

One shipment of one hundred and fifty thousand dollars, made by bootleg assayers, was identified and recovered by its rightful owners. An assayer and an engineer were arrested in possession of five thousand dollars worth of stolen ore. Convicted of grand larceny, each was fined five hundred dollars.

Shift foremen often looked the other way as miners staggered out under the weight of their loaded corset covers. Miners were hard to find for development work at twenty dollars a day — no ore yet being produced. Some miners paid up to twenty dollars a day to hold their jobs — jobs which paid less than one-fourth that in wages.

Goldfield's attitude toward crime resembled that in many frontier towns. If there was something humorous in it that could produce a laugh, it was no longer a crime. A good example came from an incident involving gambling.

George Wright lost his entire roll playing poker in Goldfield. He looked at his watch. It was close to the eleven o'clock shift change.

"Save my place," George said. "I'm going to step out a minute."

He stationed himself near an assay office. When a man came toward him with a sack on his shoulder, George shoved a stick against his ribs. "Hands up," he ordered.

The miner dropped the sack. "Now beat it," George said. He picked up the sack, took it in to the assayer, and returned to the game with twenty-seven hundred dollars in cash. The other players welcomed him back to the game with smiles and jokes about his new strike.

Suggested reading: C. B. Glasscock, *Gold in Them Hills* (Indianapolis: The Bobbs-Merrill Company, 1932).

The Two Hangings of Hootch

Joseph L. (Hootch) Simpson, pioneer in the Skidoo mining camp in California's Death Valley, liked to drink, hence his name. He was also an ornery drunk, hence his reputation as the meanest man in camp. He had a few mining claims, their titles questionable. He ran the Gold Seal saloon with Fred Oakes, and he pimped for Skidoo Babe. Many thought he had syphilis and a deranged brain. Hootch fancied himself a gunfighter. When a man called his bluff, Hootch lost part of his nose and got even meaner.

On Easter Sunday, April 19, 1908, Hootch had been on a roaring drunk for several days. He barged into Jim Arnold's Skidoo Trading Company, which had a Southern California Bank counter in the corner, and pointed his gun at the bank clerk.

"Hand over twenty dollars," he ordered. His saloon partner, Fred Oakes, and Doctor R. E. MacDonald, undismayed by the unusual holdup, disarmed Hootch. Arnold kicked him out of the store.

Hootch, reflecting on his humiliating first try at bank robbery, returned to the store and shot Jim Arnold to death. He turned his gun on Ralph Dobbs, the banker, and would have shot him if he had not been overpowered. Armed miners converged on the store from all directions.

Gordon McBain, drunk but unarmed, shouted as Hootch ran out of the store: "Don't shoot. I'll arrest him."

Doctor MacDonald, kneeling in the street with his gun at his shoulder, shouted at McBain: "Get out of the way or we'll shoot you, too."

The sheriff finally got both Hootch and McBain under arrest. He locked Hootch in a tool shed. Skidoo had no jail.

This was Skidoo's first killing, and the citizens got mad, particular when Hootch gloated over what he had done.

A group of masked men took Hootch away from the sheriff and hanged him on a telephone pole. During the investigation which followed, one joker testified that he had been awakened twenty-three times during the night to be told that Hootch had been hanged. "I was surprised every time," he told the court.

The night of Hootch's hanging had been quiet. The only sound came from McBain's iron-shod boots making ghostly thunder as he ran away. Someone had told him, "They're hanging Joe to a telephone pole. You better run like hell."

McBain took the advice and never looked back. At sunrise he was dogtrotting through Stovepipe Springs.

One man said Hootch had been a true Bohemian to the end. "At his positively last appearance, he hung around all night, as was his custom."

The idea of burying Hootch in their brand new cemetery, next to his victim, violated the sense of justice in Skidoo citizens. So Hootch's body went into a cheap pine box, dropped into an old prospect hole.

When news of the murder and lynching reached the outside, reporters and photographers came from Reno, San Francisco, and Los Angeles. Hootch had been buried two days when they arrived. They hated to return without pictures to illustrate their stories.

Primed with a few free drinks, the rougher element of the camp exhumed Hootch's body, dusted it off, and re-hung it for the press. They did this inside a large tent out of consideration for the women and children.

The mining boom in Skidoo slowed down, and Dr. MacDonald, with time on his hands, decided to see how much Hootch's syphilis had damaged his brain. He went down the prospect hole on a dark night, beheaded the corpse, and boiled the head three days to remove the flesh. Upon completion of his scientific studies, he put the skull in his office, a grisly greeter for entering patients. When the mines petered out and Skidoo was abandoned, the doctor left the skull hanging in an ore bag under his cabin floor.

Years later, another desert doctor got possession of Hootch's head. It passed from one curious person to another until it reached George Pipkin, a collector of desert relics.

What happened to Hootch's torso is not so clear. The most likely version is that Skidoo Babe, Hootch's favorite, and another lady of the evening decided to give Hootch a decent burial. They came over from Beatty, got the torso into their wagon, and started back. But it was a long, hot wagon ride through Death Valley, and their sensibilities overcame their sentiment. They ditched him somewhere along the road. What is clear is that Hootch never rested in very much peace.

Suggested reading; George C. Pipkin, *Pete Aguereberry, Death Valley Prospector and Gold Miner* (Trona: Murchison Publications, 1982).

LIFE AND COMFORT IN DEATH VALLEY

Some time in the late 1870s, Jimmy Dayton hired on as a swamper for a mule team passing through Bishop, California. The mule skinner, Ed Stiles, was freighting for the Eagle Borax Works, just starting production in Death Valley. Jimmy cooked and washed dishes, he helped feed and water the twelve-mule team, and he manned the brake on the trailing wagon. Jimmy, a small man, was a hard worker. He soon became foreman of the Greenland Ranch, later called the Furnace Creek Ranch.

By the mid 1880s the ranch, located in the pit of Death Valley, was flourishing. Jimmy's alfalfa fields grew rich and rank, providing a cutting of hay every six weeks during the season. Jimmy's heavy draft horses were so tall he had to stand on a box to fasten their collars and adjust their hames. Cattle, hogs, and sheep, grazing in his pastures, provided fresh meat for the borax mining crews, the skinners, and the swampers. Cottonwoods, willows, and palm trees grew rapidly, providing a lovely green oasis in the glaring white wastes of the valley floor.

Once each year Jimmy would collect a half-year's pay and travel to Los Angeles. He enjoyed impressing the girls with his importance as a desert rancher for the mines. But by the mid 1890s the job had lost its thrill. Only his best friend, Shorty Harris, and, sometimes, one or two other prospectors were coming by to visit. Then, on his 1897 vacation trip to Los Angeles, Jimmy fell in love. He returned to Furnace Creek with his new bride.

Jimmy's wife enjoyed the valley for the rest of the winter and the spring. That year the valley got its annual inch of rain at the right time, and it bloomed beautifully. His wife even enjoyed the social life when Shorty Harris dropped in for a visit. But when summer approached, she sadly told Jimmy, "If you want to live with me, dear, you'll have to go where there's some life and comfort."

A sad Jimmy hauled his bride to Daggett and put her on the train for Los Angeles. By late July Jimmy, who had never felt loneliness before, knew he had to follow. Jimmy took the standard precautions for summer travelers in Death Valley. In his letter of resignation he told the company exactly when he was leaving Furnace Creek and when he expected to reach Daggett. He hired an Indian to deliver the letter, paying him five dollars.

Apparently the Indian stopped in Ballarat long enough to drink up his wages. When the company got the letter, two weeks after Jimmy started out, he was already a week overdue in Daggett. The company sent two men out to look for him.

In four days they reached Bennett's Well, just twenty-two miles from Furnace Creek, with still no sign of Jimmy. Frank Tilton and Dolph Navares began wondering if Jimmy had ever left. Perhaps he had been enjoying himself in a shady place in the alfalfa field while they made their trip through hell for nothing. Then they saw the blot in the road ahead. It looked like a wagon, dancing foolishly in the shimmering heat. They whipped their weary horses ahead.

It was Jimmy's wagon alright. The dark blot in front were the four mules in his team, dead in their traces, tangled and heaped across the wagon tongue. A smaller blot at the rear of the wagon were the two led mules. Their short lead ropes tied to the end-gate held their heads up off the parched ground. But where was Jimmy?

Then Jimmy's dog, starved to a skeleton, barked weakly from a clump of mesquite. Nearby, still under the dog's loyal protection, lay Jimmy's body. Tilton and Navares, looking around, could see what had happened.

Jimmy had suddenly taken sick — perhaps sunstroke, perhaps a heart attack. He had cut the reins to his four-mule team to give them a chance on their own. He had either forgotten the two led mules or he was unable to get back to them. But his old instinct as a swamper had made him set the brake when he stopped. The team could not pull the wagon, and Jimmy had not unhitched them. They died in harness, milling and struggling in an agony of heat and thirst.

Jimmy had crawled to the mesquite clump, knowing that he was dying. It also appeared that the starving dog had fought off coyotes, as they tried to reach the body of its master.

Tilton and Navares went on Furnace Creek Ranch, taking the dog with them. They took boards off a barn and made a coffin. They returned to their gruesome job with a tarpaulin and two shovels.

Jimmy had been dead at least two weeks. The men dug a grave, pushed and rolled Jimmy's body on to the tarpaulin, lifted him into the coffin, and lowered it into the ground.

"Well, Jimmy," Tilton said, "you lived in the heat and you died in the heat, and after what you been through I guess you ought to be comfortable in hell."

Suggested reading: C. B. Glasscock, *Here's Death Valley* (New York: Grosset & Dunlap, 1940).

JIMMY DAYTON IN DEATH VALLEY

SINGLE-BLANKET, JACKASS PROSPECTOR

Frank Harris, born in Rhode Island in 1857, never got much over five feet tall, so he was always called Shorty. His father, a shoemaker, died in poverty when Shorty was seven. Shorty went to live with an aunt. He ran away at eleven to work in textile mills. The village priest taught him to read and write. Otherwise his only school was the alley.

At nineteen Shorty crawled out of a boxcar in Dodge City, Kansas, to see stacks of buffalo hides, to hear bellowing cattle, chippies, gamblers, and cowhands, and to recognize a chance for young men who had come out of alleys. He met Wyatt Earp and a thin fellow with a cough who, if he liked you, would go to hell for you — Doc Holliday, the coldest killer in the west. He also met a percentage girl in one of the saloons — a lovely girl, not altogether bad. He fell in love.

"Shorty," she said, "don't be a sucker. Go on west. You might find a good claim."

"I'm broke,"

She thrust some bills into his pocket.

"I don't live off girls," he protested.

"Go on now and good luck, Shorty."

He rode freights on west, arriving in California on the same train that carried U. S. Grant. The general, on a speaking tour, had a private car; Shorty rode the rods below. He worked in Los Angeles, and then heard about big gold strikes in Colorado. He rode freights back to Leadville.

He found luck in Leadville. He sold out for fifteen thousand. The mine produced millions. Within a week he was penniless, and had many Leadville friends.

"All I've got to do is find another gulch," he told them.

Shorty sold his second claim to Horace Tabor. He remembered the girl in Dodge City. He returned there for wining, dining, and dancing. Then new friends gathered around, and in a week Shorty was broke again.

When he went down to the freight yard to steal a ride on the rods, he saw the girl. He begged her to marry him.

"Shorty, you don't know anything about my past, and you still want to marry me?" she asked.

"You don't know nothing about my past, either."

But the girl insisted and Shorty headed to the Coeur d' Alene in Idaho. Drifting on to Montana, Utah, and Arizona, Shorty finally settled in Nevada and the Death Valley area of California.

He discovered or shared in the discovery of five rich mines. Each time he sold out too quickly and too cheaply. Whenever Shorty was in the money, he couldn't do enough for his friends. He'd buy food, set up the drinks, and make grubstake loans until he was broke again.

His golden odyssey began on March 17, 1892, in the Panamint Mountains of California. He named the mine the St. Patrick in honor of the day. He sold out for seven thousand dollars, which was soon spent setting up the drinks for friends.

Then he found copper at Greenwater, but that discovery produced nothing, as his partner got drunk and forgot to file the claims.

Shorty's discovery of the Bullfrog mine in 1904, which launched the town of Rhyolite, Nevada, brought him nine hundred dollars and three barrels of whiskey. Within a few months, adjoining owners refused to sell for a million dollars. That discovery brought two railroads into Rhyolite, and gave jobs to thousands of men, but Shorty only had a hangover and many thanks.

After he discovered the Harrisburg mine, Shorty sold out for thirty-five thousand shares of stock in the company created to produce the gold. Then the majority owner levied a cash assessment of ten cents a share on the stock, which Shorty could not pay. He lost everything, and wasn't even able to set up the drinks.

His last discovery was at Skidoo. Shorty often said that he had been leaded at Leadville, crippled at Cripple Creek, and rawhided out of Rawhide.

Ballarat, the commercial center of Death Valley, flourished for about the first twenty years of this century. Shorty made Ballarat his headquarters for supplies and entertainment. There he met the Belle of Ballarat, Bessie Hart. She was over six feet tall and weighed in at two hundred ten. She could whip her weight in wildcats or wild men. Shorty — all five feet of him — fell in love with Bessie.

One day, while Shorty was sharpening steel in the Ballarat blacksmith shop, and his heart's desire worked the bellows, he decided to speak up.

"Bessie, let's you and me get married."

Bessie, surprised, stopped the bellows. The charcoal glow died away while she looked down at Shorty as if seeing him for the first time. She looked him over carefully, not unkindly but with an appraising look. Finally she spoke.

SHORTY HARRIS' PROSPECTING PARTNER

"You're a damn good man, Shorty. You're a fine friend and I like you. But as a husband? No dice, my dear. You're just too small for a damn big job!"

Shorty didn't argue. He stayed a bachelor the rest of his life. He spent most of his last year in the ruins of Ballarat, by then a ghost town.

When Shorty was old a friend interviewing him asked if he would be a prospector if he had his life to live over. "I wouldn't change places with the president," Shorty said. "My only regret is that I didn't start sooner. When I go out, every time my foot touches the ground, I think before the sun goes down I'll be worth ten million.'"

"But you never get the money," the interviewer said.

"Who in the hell wants ten million dollars? It's the game, man — the game."

In November, 1934, Shorty, seventy-eight, lay dying in Big Pine, California, after a building collapsed on him. A 79-year old friend arrived. He had traveled over four hundred miles to reach Shorty. They talked a while. Then the friend, Pete Harmon who had known Shorty in Leadville, stood up and shook out the contents of a small canvas sack. He had a few dimes and nickels and two bills, a twenty and a one.

"Shorty, I'm eatin' regular now and got a little besides. I reckon you're kinda shy. You take this."

"No, Pete. I'm doing just fine."

Shorty died before the year was out. Friends came to the funeral from as far away as Reno and Los Angeles. It was the largest gathering of people in Death Valley. The hearse, coming from Big Pine, was delayed by prospectors along the road, who wanted one last goodbye with their friend. They wanted to honor their uncrowned king, but they were unable to be reverent or sentimental about it. They dug the grave to fit their short friend, forgetting that the coffin would be regular in length. The internment had to be held up while they lengthened the grave.

Shorty had asked to be buried next to his friend, Jim Dayton, buried where he had died thirty-five years before. He also specified what he wanted for an epitaph. Both wishes were met. The epitaph reads, "Here lies Shorty Harris, a Single-Blanket, Jackass Prospector."

Suggested reading: Frank Shorty Harris, "Chasing Rainbows" in Richard E. Lingenfelter, *Death Valley Lore* (Reno: University of Nevada Press, 1988).

TWO WOMEN IN THE KLONDIKE

George Carmack had hunted gold in the Yukon River Valley for years. He lived with a Tagish-Tlinglit woman until she died of influenza. Following Tagish custom he joined up with his first woman's younger sister, who had lost her Tlinglit man and their infant daughter in the same epidemic. George called his second woman Kate. In a few years they had their own daughter, Graphie Grace. Kate's skill at finding food, snaring animals, and making clothing helped George in his prospecting.

On August 16, 1896, George and Kate, along with Kate's brother, Skookum Jim, and her nephew, Dawson Charlie, were camped on Rabbit Creek, a tributary of the Klondike River. They saw the sun shining on a yellow strip of metal, so wide in its bed rock it reminded George of a thick cheese sandwich. By the end of the month the creek was renamed Bonanza Creek, and every inch of it had been staked and claimed.

Clarence Berry, the first man to hear Carmack's news, was tending bar at McPhee's saloon when Carmack swaggered in, bragging of his discovery. Berry dropped his bar rag and ran home to his wife, Ethel.

"They hit it big up on Rabbit Crick," he said. "I'll take the rowboat up to stake us a couple claims. You put together what we need for the winter."

Ethel had been Mrs. Berry for five months. She started assembling five tons of provisions. Clarence returned in a few days to record their claims.

"I'm going back down in the rowboat," he said. "You get the stuff on the steamer and follow."

Ethel had just twelve hours to get their provisions to the steamer dock. She made it. Their claims, the first staked and recorded after the discovery claims, turned out to be among the richest on the Klondike.

Clarence Berry, like George Carmack, had been hunting gold in the Yukon River Valley for years without success. The previous fall, after spending two years away from his California home, he had gone "outside" to see Ethel. She would not let her fiance return north alone. She put together a trousseau of warm, strong material that would stand up in the harsh land of the midnight sun. They married in March, 1896, and headed north for their Yukon honeymoon. It took them nine weeks to get from Juneau to Forty Mile over the steep climb that would later be famous as the Chilkoot Trail.

When they had reached Forty Mile, Charlie left immediately for a five-week prospecting trip that seemed an eternity to Ethel.

"There was absolutely nothing to do," she wrote. "No one who has not had a like experience could appreciate even half the misery contained in those words — nothing to do. Just imagine sitting for hours in one's home doing nothing, looking out a scrap of a window and seeing nothing, searching for work and finding nothing. At times when I felt I could not bear another minute the utter blankness of such an existence, I would walk to a little cemetery nearby for consolation."

When Clarence returned he decided to stay closer to home, so he was the first to hear Carmack's news.

Winter mining was hard. They sank shafts to bedrock and stockpiled gold-bearing gravel until spring when water would be available to wash it out.

Housekeeping was just as hard. Ethel no longer complained about having nothing to do.

"We could not get one drop of water without first melting the ice, which necessitated keeping a fire all day," Ethel wrote. "Keeping the fire is enough to occupy the whole of one person's time."

In the tradition of the North, hospitality was extended to visitors at all hours. On one occasion, ten men showed up just as Ethel and Clarence were starting dinner. Ethel had to cook another entire dinner, this one much larger.

"We didn't think about games or amusements," she said. "It was just work, eat, and sleep."

The next July, when the steamer *Portland* tied up at the Seattle docks, Ethel stood on deck in a ragged dress, wearing shoes with many holes but no laces. The bedroll at the feet of the poor farm girl was too heavy for her to lift. It contained a hundred thousand dollars worth of gold!

The *Portland* brought the first news of the Klondike discovery. Ethel's story, "The bride of the Klondike," ran in newspapers all over the world. A few months before, she had huddled in a small cabin with a dirt floor and a flour-sack window, panning gold by lamplight in the same washtub she and Clarence used for their baths. Now she answered questions fired at her by reporters who were eager to tell the story of one of the world's great gold discoveries.

"What advice would you give women who would go north?" they asked.

"Don't go." She smiled. "It's a hard life."

But Ethel and Clarence returned the next spring, this time with Ethel's younger sister, Edna. They worked hard and soon had rich claims in Alaska, near Fairbanks. Then they started large-scale dredging near Circle.

Ethel and Clarence returned north every year until Clarence died in 1930. The wealthy widow lived in Beverly Hills until her death in 1948.

At first life did not change for Kate Carmack. She made her first trip outside with George in 1898. They had $150,000 in gold to be shared between the original discoverers. George signed Kate into hotels as his wife and proudly draped gold nugget necklaces around her neck.

But the three Tagish were bewildered at the crowds and traffic. They drank too much. Newspaper reporters, more interested in colorful stories than factual ones, wrote about wild, ignorant savages from the northland. When George introduced Kate and her family to his Baptist, non-drinking sister in California, the culture clash began. Kate spent the winter trying to conform to her sister-in-law's ideas of proper lady-like conduct. She failed. The Tagish all followed George back north the next spring, but Graphie Gracie stayed behind for more of her aunt's civilizing.

When they returned south the next July, the *Seattle Post-Intelligencer* reported that "Mrs. George Carmack, the Indian wife of the discoverer of the Klondike, slept last night in the city jail, charged with being drunk and disorderly." She was arrested "while executing an aboriginal Yukon war dance in the second floor corridor of the Seattle Hotel."

George had had enough. He took Kate's relatives back north, but he left Kate with his sister for more civilizing. Then, enjoying Dawson's high life, he proposed to an American businesswoman with gold experience in Africa and Australia and several broken marriages of her own behind her. Paying off his partners in the Yukon was easy, but Kate wanted to fight. She wanted a divorce, but learned that she had no marriage to be divorced from. She eventually filed for support for Gracie and "palimony" for herself, but she was decades ahead of her time. Two years had passed when she dropped the suit and returned north. Her brother built her a cabin, and paid for Gracie's schooling. Kate sold needlework to tourists and posed for pictures.

George never sent a dime to either Kate or their daughter. To add insult to injury, he persuaded Gracie to leave her mission school and join him and his new wife in Seattle. The loss was devastating to Kate, who held the Tagish belief that children belong to the mother's clan. She died of influenza in 1920.

Suggested reading: Frances Backhouse, *Women of the Klondike*, (Vancouver: Whitecap Books, 1996).

KING OF THE KLONDIKE

Alex McDonald, an enormous Scotsman from Nova Scotia, had spent fourteen years in Colorado silver mines before moving north to Juneau. He went on to the Klondike after the 1896 gold strike.

McDonald had no money, but his experience as a land buyer for the Alaska Commercial Company gave him a shrewd sense of land values in the north. His faith in the future of owning land amounted to a religion.

With ham-sized hands and a body to match, McDonald moved and talked slowly, but he was not slow-witted. He bought half of a gold claim for a sack of flour and a side of bacon. Later the claim showed a forty-foot-wide pay streak where one man could pan out five thousand dollars a day.

Most men would have been content with a half interest in such a rich mine, but the Big Moose from Antigonish had a burning drive to acquire more property. He introduced the "lay" system into the Klondike. He would lease out a lay or strip of a claim, defined as a certain width and limited to a specific time period. The lessee would then mine that area for that time, sharing his recovery with Big Alex. McDonald would use his share to acquire interests in other claims. Within a year he was hailed as the King of the Klondike, the richest man there, perhaps the richest in the world.

McDonald's statement of business affairs, made to get a loan from the Canadian Bank of Commerce, was a classic of the north country. It took the whole banking staff several hours to extract full information from the slow-speaking man. Each time he was about to sign the deposition listing his assets, he would put down the pen, rub his huge jowls and say, "I just remembered another claim." The list finally showed fifty mining properties. He borrowed a huge sum to buy another claim. Before the summer was over, he had paid the loan off and pocketed an equal amount as profit.

McDonald was the biggest investor and had the biggest investment in the Yukon Telegraph Company. He owned two stern-wheeler steamers for shipping on the Yukon. He owned a fifteen-mule pack train to haul the gold from his many claims into Dawson City.

Big Alex always called gold, "trash." To him it was only useful to buy land.

Alex built his own building, the McDonald, in Dawson City. He lived on the first floor, where he kept a bowl filled with forty-five pounds of large gold nuggets. When Alice Henderson, a newspaper correspondent, dropped in, Alex waved at the bowl.

"Help yourself to some nuggets," he said, as though offering chocolates. "Take some of the bigger ones."

Alice hesitated.

"Go ahead," Alex insisted. "Take as many as you like. They mean nothing to me. There are lots more, anyway."

McDonald made a memorable trip to Paris, Rome and London in 1898. He had an audience with the Pope, who made him a Knight of St. Gregory for his philanthropy to Father William Judge's hospital in Dawson City. He went on to London for his first ride in an elevator. There he met and married Margaret Chisholm, twenty-year-old daughter of the superintendent of the Thames Water Police.

Big Alex had become the leader of Dawson City's Four Hundred. The townspeople asked him to preside at the farewell celebration in 1899, when Sam Steele, Superintendent of the Mounties, left the Yukon. Alex had carefully rehearsed for several days what was supposed to be a graceful farewell speech, to be given as he handed a bag of gold to Steele. At the last minute the King of the Klondike lumbered forward, thrust the bag into Steele's hands, and blurted out, "Here, Sam — here's a poke for you. Good-bye."

In spite of that performance, Big Alex was chosen to present a bucket of nuggets to Lady Minto, wife of Canada's governor-general, when the viceregal party visited Dawson. When the moment arrived, the King of the Klondike shoved the bucket toward Her Ladyship with his great, ham hands, saying, "Here. Take it. It's only trash."

But the good times didn't last. McDonald spent his last years prospecting on Clearwater Creek, far from the rich claims on Bonanza and El Dorado Creeks. One day another prospector found his body lying by the chopping-block at the little cabin Big Alex was using. He had died of a heart attack while splitting wood.

Sometime before, he had bought a life insurance policy, so the widow of the King of the Klondike was able to live in some comfort.

Suggested reading: Pierre Berton, *The Klondike Fever* (New York: Alfred A. Knopf, 1958).

STAMPEDER

Prospectors searching for instant riches are great stampeders. Word of a new strike on another creek, or over a mountain range, or in a distant country starts a rush of dream-filled people. Most were men and most of the dreams were about returning home to buy or build bigger farms, businesses, or professional practices. But a few stampeders were women, and for one of them the dream was very different. Nellie Cashman, probably the greatest stampeder of them all, wanted to share wealth with others, usually her beloved Catholic Church.

The Irish potato famine forced Nellie, her widowed mother, and her little sister from County Cork to Boston when Nellie was about five. In 1865, when Nellie was twenty, they moved on to San Francisco. Seven years later, with her sister married, Nellie took her mother to Pioche, Nevada, and opened a boarding house. One of the most violent mining camps in the West, Pioche averaged a street killing a month. Nellie was soon active in Catholic charities.

But the boom days were over, and Nellie returned to San Francisco. A year later she heard the call again, this time from the Cassair District of Northern British Columbia. She opened a boarding house and grubstaked prospectors there in summer 1874. She also prospected herself, which was much more exciting.

On her way out for the winter, she learned that hundreds of miners had been trapped by winter's sudden onslaught. Knowing they faced scurvy and starvation, Nellie bought provisions, hired six men to help, and hurried back north. With snow too deep for dogs, each person had to pull a sled. Sometimes they moved only five miles a day. One night Nellie was buried under an avalanche. Another time she was lost for twenty-eight hours, without shelter or blankets. They reached the trapped miners in February, saving them from certain death. Nellie nursed them back to health and became part of northern folklore. Later that year she gathered contributions from miners to help the Sisters of St. Ann build a hospital.

But by 1876 that boom was off, and Nellie, after visiting her mother and sister in San Francisco, headed for Tucson. Not for gold or silver — they hadn't been discovered yet. She probably thought it would become a transportation center. At any rate, she had learned that, besides being attractive, she

NELLIE CASHMAN

British Columbia Archives

was generous, afraid of nothing, and could lead the way in a man's part of the world. Arizona would be her oyster!

She ran restaurants, boarding houses, and clothing stores in Tucson, Tombstone, and Bisbee. After Ed Schieffelin discovered silver, she enjoyed the greater excitement of prospecting. She also helped the Catholic Church raise money to build a hospital and a church.

In 1881 Nellie's brother-in-law died. She took in her sister and five nieces and nephews, all under ten. But charitable work, running several businesses, occasionally prospecting, and helping raise five children was not enough. Nellie needed a bigger challenge.

It came in 1883, with news that gold had been found on the Baja California Peninsula. Nellie organized twenty-one men into an expedition to travel over a thousand miles by stage, railroad, ship, and burro to the new bonanza. These weren't ordinary men. One was a Cochise County commissioner; another would become a United States senator. But Nellie was the boss. Wearing her customary black trousers, blue shirt, and high-topped boots, she made the decisions and gave the orders.

She failed, but her effort brought even more fame than her rescue work had in British Columbia. Nellie, who would later walk twenty-one miles alone on an arctic trail in sixty-one below zero weather, met her match in Mexico. In deserts so hot even lizards avoided them, she and a few of her men nearly perished. But she turned around and got all her party back to safety, while men in nearby parties died of thirst.

Nellie returned to Tombstone. She tried New Mexico and other mining camps in Arizona, but business, charity, and family (most of the children had been farmed out to various catholic schools) did not provide the excitement this intrepid woman needed. The *Arizona Daily Star* reported in November, 1897, that she was trying to organize a gold mining company to go to Alaska. "Her many friends in Arizona will wish her success, for during her twenty years residence in the territory she has made several fortunes, all of which have gone to charity."

She could not raise the party, but she went anyway. In spring 1898 Nellie got off the boat at Skagway, looked up at the Chilkoot Pass, and knew she had been challenged. Dawson was six hundred miles away. A young person in good condition could reach the top of the pass on a good day in about seven hours. But Nellie was fifty-four, and the Mounties required everyone to have at least nine hundred pounds of supplies, enough to last a year. It took Nellie three weeks to get it all up to the pass. With a heavy sled, pulled by one dog, she moved on north.

She reached Dawson in April. By September she was working four claims and had a tomato can full of gold dust. She also ran a restaurant and helped the Sisters of St. Ann build a hospital, just as she had twenty-three years before.

Nellie recovered a hundred thousand dollars from one claim, but spent it buying other claims. She continued to prospect, working on snowshoes and with dog teams. By 1904 Dawson was one of the largest cities in the northern part of the world. It had four newspapers, three hospitals, and forty restaurants.

But the boom was off, and Nellie heard of a strike on the Chena River, where the camp of Fairbanks was starting. There she operated a grocery store and a miners' supply house. This time the hospital was being built by an Episcopal mission. Nellie, as broad-minded and she was generous, twisted miners' arms as before.

Her weather-beaten, freckled face creased into a maze of wrinkles as she said, "Okay boys, this is for the hospital. You've all had the good of it, you low-down, blankety-blank varmints — and if you got money to throw away at poker, you can give it to them hard working Christian women that's taking care of the sick."

In July 1905 Nellie headed up the Koyukuk River, far to the north of Fairbanks. That gold discovery was north of the Arctic Circle, the farthest north of any mines in the world. The ground had to be thawed out by boilers before it could be worked. There she prospected, ran restaurants, and raised money for the next twenty years. She also served as a deputy United States marshal. Nellie went outside every winter to escape the days when the sun never appeared.

Her last winter outside was 1923-24. In spring 1924 she got within eighty miles of her claims, but could go no further. The years of meeting challenges had taken their toll. She retreated southward from one hospital to another (most of which she had helped build) until she reached St. Ann's at Victoria. She held on until January 1925. She died of pneumonia at St. Ann's, aged seventy-nine.

Suggested reading: Don Chaput, *Nellie Cashman* (Tucson: Westernlore Press, 1995.)

ORDERING INFORMATION

True Tales of the Old West is projected for several volumes.

Proposed titles include:

Warriors and Chiefs	In print
Soldiers	In print
Native Women	In print
Mountain Men	In print
Pioneer Women	In print
Ranchers and Cowboys	In print
Horses and Riders	In print
Miners	In Print
Entertainers	In print
Frontiersmen	Soon to appear
Law Enforcers	Soon to appear
Outlaws	Soon to appear
Writers	Under way
Scouts	Under way
Homesteaders	Under way
Dogs and Masters	Under way
Explorers	Under way
Lawyers & Judges	Under way
Railroaders	Started
Merchants	Started
Army Women	Started

Ask at your bookstore or write:

PIONEER PRESS
Box 216
Carson City, NV 89702-0216